To Tell the
Sacred Tale

Spiritual Direction and Narrative

Janet K. Ruffing, RSM

PAULIST PRESS
New York/Mahwah, NJ

Cover and book design by Lynn Else

Library of Congress Cataloging-in-Publication Data

Ruffing, Janet, 1945-
    To tell the sacred tale : spiritual direction and narrative / Janet K. Ruffing.
        p. cm.
    Includes bibliographical references (p.   ).
    ISBN 978-0-8091-4723-6 (alk. paper)
    1. Spiritual direction—Christianity. 2. Storytelling—Religious aspects—Christianity. I. Title.
    BV5053.R84 2010
    253.5'3—dc22

                                                                    2010042907

Published by Paulist Press
997 Macarthur Boulevard
Mahwah, New Jersey 07430

www.paulistpress.com

Printed and bound in the
United States of America

Contents

For my spiritual-direction students these last twenty-five years and my directees, who never fail to amaze me with their stories of God and their dedication to ministry and life in God...
...as well as to my co-supervisors at Fordham: Patricia Cowley, OP; Dr. Fredrica Halligan; Dr. Beverly Musgrave; Margaret Ellen Burke, SC; Dr. Mary Byrne; Kathryn King, FSP; Dr. Robert Giugliano; Vivienne Joyce, SC; and Mary Naughton

Acknowledgments

This manuscript began twenty-five years ago as my doctoral dissertation. At the time, I had five or six years of experience as a spiritual director and more than ten years as a directee. I had not yet begun teaching spiritual direction at Fordham.

I remain grateful for the many spiritual directors and retreat directors who have listened to me tell my sacred tale and who have become, indeed, beloved companions on a journey of grace over the years. I discovered in the process how much I needed to tell my own sacred tale in spiritual direction in order to fully receive the grace discovered and to respond more deeply to its implications for life and ministry. Now, after twenty-five years of mentoring spiritual directors—initially at Mercy Center, in Burlingame, California, and then these many years at Fordham University—I am deeply grateful to the many students who have shared their own stories of spiritual direction with me, especially Sam, Mary, Ellen, Krista, Kevin, Linda, Charles, Evelyn, and Opal, whose stories or reflections I have used in this volume with their gracious permission. Their names have been changed, as have their directors' names, to protect their confidentiality.

These accounts about spiritual direction span my time in the field from the mid-1980s through fall of 2008. I have enjoyed working in a multicultural environment since my doctoral studies in Berkeley in the 1980s and subsequently at Fordham University. I have learned so much from my international students, who have been shaped by their wisdom stories that so many of them have shared with me. I am also grateful to my initial group of interviewees, whose insights I retained in this volume.

I am grateful to my editors at Paulist Press for the relationship they have maintained with me through three previous manuscripts and for patiently waiting for me to complete this one, which we planned together nine years ago. Editor Kathleen Walsh was still with Paulist Press at that time and gave me excellent guidance. Academic editor Christopher Bellitto's suggestions for this new volume have been both supportive and skillful. Then managing editor Paul McMahon and the late Larry Boadt, CSP, then president and publisher, became old friends and wonderful collaborators.

This writing project has grown organically out of my teaching, and Fordham University and the Graduate School of Religion and Religious Education graciously supported me with a faculty fellowship and the release from teaching that accompanies it. I am also grateful for Vivienne Joyce, SC, Dr. Robert Giugliano, and Nunzio Gubitosa who taught the practicum in spiritual direction without me so I could write.

During the writing process itself, I am grateful for the beauty of Mercy Center, Madison, Connecticut, nestled as it is on the Long Island Sound. Walks along the beach and in the neighborhood, as well as contemplative time each day, were enormously renewing. The Sisters of Mercy there—Florence Trahan, Mary Daly, and Judy Fortune—welcomed me into their community and were fine companions during this time. In addition to my own RSM community, Joan Linley and the rest of the staff at Mercy Center have been both welcoming and enjoyable to be with; they also offered me lovely writing space.

I am also deeply grateful to Marilyn Gouailhardou, RSM, for the gift of her expert proofreading of my manuscript and her many years of friendship and support since she first taught me in high school, many years ago.

Feast of St. Catherine of Siena
April 29, 2009

Our Stories

It is our stories
our sacred, chaotic, blessed stories,
our awe-drenched, doubting, joyous stories:
it is our stories
that are the stones
of God's language
on the rocky, jagged, radiant
path of life.
It is the holy listener
who helps arrange these stones
into cairns
which point the way to God's desire for our lives
and
God's desire for our every moment.
The cairns, if patiently balanced,
uneven though they be,
if patiently balanced,
can point the way to heaven.
Heaven, after all,
is making God-serving meaning of our stories
on this rocky, jagged, radiant
path of life.

—Jennifer Hoffman
from *Listen*, 3.1 (January 2009)

Preface

"It is our stories," as Jennifer Hoffman says, "which point the way to God's desire for our lives and God's desire for our every moment." When we hear ourselves tell our own sacred tales, we discover more clearly what God's desires are for us and ours for God. This volume began with *Uncovering Stories of Faith: Spiritual Direction and Narrative*, published in 1989. Since that first attempt to understand spiritual direction as essentially a narrative practice, I have made many new discoveries about the importance of narrative in spiritual direction.

My extensive experience with international students for more than two decades continues to remind me that many third-world cultures still prefer oral histories and oral narratives to transmit knowledge across generations and to share experiences—even though the people are also literate. Consequently, a narrative approach to spiritual direction is the most accessible paradigm for spiritual direction in the third world. Within such oral cultures, spiritual directors are more likely to respond to their directees' sacred tales with another story, rather than respond to their directees' story directly.

In addition to taking a more global focus beyond first-world culture into account, I address the dominance of postmodernism in Western countries as a pervasive worldview that profoundly affects how we understand ourselves. This has resulted in an increase in the need for telling personal stories in general and especially in spiritual direction. In other parts of the world, however, everyone is affected by globalization but not necessarily by postmodernism. As chapter 2 demonstrates, we continue to live in a conflict of interpretation about what kind of a story we have fallen into.

Is the present antimodern, modern, or postmodern? There are people of faith in all three positions. The experience of God is dramatically different depending on how influenced a person is by one or another of these interpretations. Many Western people vacillate between postmodern and late-modern points of view. But even in the West, there is a significant number of people who try to isolate themselves within an antimodern religious community.

Personal identity has always developed in relationship both to a culture's dominant stories and the stories each of us tells ourselves. We now understand this narrative impulse of humans as a universal feature of experience, rooted in neuroscience and in intersubjective experience. The Western sense of self as autonomous in the extreme tends to deny current psychological understandings that we are all essentially selves in relation; and in Asian and African cultures, also rooted in the "we" of a community as well. Some theorists use neuroscience to undermine belief in religion or faith while others use it in the service of belief and faith.

This book is an organic outgrowth from my first book. There have been exciting developments in narrative theory, in the field of spiritual direction, and in neuropsychology that dramatically enhance our understandings of the significance of personal storytelling in the context of spiritual direction. The introduction highlights some of the reasons why narrative remains important in spiritual direction. It places this ministry within the Christian tradition and offers a historical overview of various models of spiritual direction and how each model affects the kind of story told in spiritual direction. Throughout the rest of the text, references are made to the expansion of spiritual direction to include interfaith relationships as well as interdenominational relationships. Although I kept my original stories of spiritual direction, this volume has been expanded with stories and examples from six other directees who gave me their stories within the last five or six years, and some within the last year.

Chapters 2 through the conclusion have been substantially changed and expanded. Chapter 2 complements the interpersonal, conversational model of hermeneutics with considerations by David Tracy and Johannes Baptist Metz that discuss our characterization of the present moment, God's return in the postmodern context, and the claim of the "other" and of suffering humanity on us. Especially important is the recognition of formerly "non-persons" who become persons through authoring their own stories. What *non-person* means in this context will become clear in chapter 2.

Chapter 3 retains much from the first version, but significantly modifies Stephen Crites's groundbreaking understanding of narrative and experience in view of new work in neuroscience, which is then discussed more extensively in chapter 4. Many fresh case examples are given to illustrate this material on the narrative impulse, as well as new material from Kathleen Fischer not only on imagery but on feelings in spiritual direction. I have also added a more nuanced description of the emergent quality of images and words in spiritual direction.

Chapter 4 dramatically expands literary critical material on narrative using material from neuroscience, which allows us to better understand the narrative impulse in human experience as it relates to a variety of ways our sense of self develops somatically, relationally, and autobiographically. The work of Ulric Neisser and Antonio Damasio provides exciting new insights about how the autobiographical self is based on embodiment. Postmodern literary theory suggests that the self is nothing but words, texts, endlessly in flux, fragmented, and constantly changing. I challenge the helpfulness of this view and offer reflections by personality theorists such as Dan McAdams and others who contest this extreme view of flux in the self in favor of the desirability of continuity of character, as well as change and transformation. I give more explicit attention to metaphors of the self in spiritual autobiographical writing, which also apply to its oral form in spiritual direction. I have added work by theologian John S. Dunne to nuance, as he says, how God is involved in "telling me the story of my journey in time." I have also added an entirely new section on the discernment of stories.

Chapter 5 has retained much from the original. However, as in chapter 4, it really does matter how we tell our story and how, in the telling of one story, we often get another. There is new material from developmental psychologist Ronald Irwin, who proposes a need to understand human existence beyond an ego-generated identity. His developmental approach points to a quality of consciousness that is open to self-transcendence and offers a way of understanding spiritual or meditative experience beyond ego alone. The section on telling stories of God contains much of the original text but has been expanded with insights from Neisser and Damasio about experiences that happen in the body and in image rather than in language.

The conclusion has been developed and expanded with material from contemporary literary writers about how stories affect those who read or hear them, which strengthens an understanding of the influence that directees have on their directors, as well as how public stories of belief affect their readers. Finally, rich new case material illuminates the interrelationship between the directee's story of spiritual direction and the director's experience.

Finally, most chapters have been enhanced with questions for further reflection intended particularly for spiritual directors.

Introduction
The Story Begins

> So abounding will that joy be that it will follow you to bed at night and rise with you in the morning. It will pursue you through the day in everything you do....The joy and the desire will seem to be part of each other...though you will be at a loss to say just what it is that you long for. Your whole self will be transformed; your face will shine with an inner beauty; and for as long as you feel it, nothing will sadden you. A thousand miles would you run to speak with another who you knew really felt it and yet when you got there, find yourself speechless! And yet your only joy would be to speak of it...words fruitful, and filled with fire.[1]

This quotation, from the fourteenth-century spiritual classic *The Book of Privy Counseling*, captures the ambivalence, joy, and desire of men and women who experience their deep longings for God and want to talk about it with someone else who "really feels" it. Such seekers—who are touched by the holy Mystery in some way, or who recognize there is "something more" in life that they wish to explore, seek, or welcome—often look for a spiritual director to help them. Contemporary spiritual writer Tilden Edwards puts it this way:

> We yearn for a soul-friend with whom we can share our desire for the Holy One and with whom we can try to identify and embrace the hints of divine Presence and invitation in our lives. Neither soul-friends nor anyone else can fully enter our deep

> soul space. However, they can listen to our articula-
> tions of it, silently open these to God as soon as
> they are heard, and occasionally speak when some-
> thing is heard in that openness that seems to be
> meant for the directee.[2]

Experiences of transcendence and hints of divine Presence challenge, allure, and invite personal response to the myste- rious Other, who draws near in the concrete circumstances of their lives.[3] Although some never seek the assistance of a trusted other with the religious dimension of their lives, oth- ers long for such companionship.

The Western Christian tradition calls this process of encouraging another's spiritual development "spiritual direc- tion" and the person who offers this help a "spiritual director." Within this tradition, spiritual direction is one of the primary spiritual practices that helps the directee with a personal understanding of the spiritual life, growth in self-knowledge, and deepening intimacy with God.

Although spiritual direction has been described in many ways, from my perspective, telling the unique story of God and self—telling one's sacred tale—is the central activity that occurs in spiritual direction. The only access spiritual direc- tors have to another's experience is through the way directees enact and represent it in their stories. When directees express their religious experience, they must pay greater attention to the details of that experience through reflecting on, remembering, and recollecting features from "the totality of the unreflected-on...primary experience."[4] In doing so, directees re-present and even enact the event they have already organized in a preliminary way. The use of narrative makes the experience live again for directees, even as it allows the director to share it. This storying leads directees to reflect on the meaning and implication of the original experience as the director shapes directees' stories of God and self in the interaction between the director and directee. The director's response to the directee's stories profoundly affects the directee's narratives. Directees thus represent

2

themselves in the way they want to be known and understood by this director in this very particular context of telling their sacred tales.[5]

Historically, spiritual direction has taken many different forms, exhibiting both change and continuity over its long history. Although the historical models of spiritual direction vary, spiritual direction as a practice has remained constant in Christian tradition. A survey of the historical models of spiritual direction can enhance our understanding of how each model or type affects the relationship between director and directee and shapes the story told in that model. In particular instances, each of these models may still be operative in some religious groups and cultures.

Typological History of Spiritual Direction

A brief exploration of six successive models of spiritual direction will provide historical context for the discussion of the narrative activity in the contemporary spiritual-direction conversation.[6] These typological models include the fourth-century desert *abbas* and *ammas*, the Benedictine monastic model, the late-medieval non-monastic model, the sixteenth-century Ignatian-interventionist model, the seventeenth- to nineteenth-century post-Tridentine director of conscience, and the Vatican II contemporary model.

The Desert *Abbas* and *Ammas*

The desert tradition of spiritual direction emerged in the fourth and fifth centuries in Egypt, Palestine, and Syria as a model of spiritual guidance distinct from the ordinary pastoral care of Christians. Because of the isolation and harshness of life in the wilderness, and because of "casualties" among those who rashly attempted a solitary search for God in the depths of their hearts, the need for guidance became extremely acute. Newcomers to desert life began to seek out an *abba* or *amma* to guide them, an elder seasoned by soli-tude with an experiential knowledge of the gifts and tempta-tions of this lifestyle and of the life of prayer. The neophyte would either live with the elder or nearby.

The title *abba* ("father") or *amma* ("mother") reflected the preferred nature of the relationship and was based on the experience of spiritual paternity or maternity that character-ized this wholly charismatic and freely chosen relationship.[7] This graced ability to facilitate the unfolding life of the Spirit in one's spiritual son or daughter depended on the disposi-tions of the seeker, the discerning "word," and the example of the elder. Theologian André Louf describes the necessary dis-positions of the seeker as "a sincere desire to know God's will and the beginning of detachment from all selfish desire."[8] These dispositions enabled the seeker to approach the *abba* or *amma* and ask for a "word" of life. This "word," unique to each seeker, functioned as a "sacramental." Its purpose lay in revealing and healing a seeker's particular weaknesses or deficiencies.[9] More than information or instruction, this "word" provided a way toward God. As such, it "was not to be discussed or analyzed or disputed in any way; at times, it was not even understood; but it was to be memorized and absorbed into life."[10]

The seeker's relationship to the spiritual parent also implied docility, obedience, and trust. He or she entrusted all interior movements of the heart to the elder for spiritual dis-cernment. This manifestation of the heart was distinct from sacramental confession, which was rarely practiced during this period. Manifestation of the heart helped the neophytes become aware of the abiding tendencies and dispositions of their hearts, what tempted them and which passions most confused or deceived them in their quest for God. This dia-logue included not only interior movements, but also the pre-cise details about daily life in the cell. Its goal was to enhance spiritual freedom and eventually engender the deep peace that results from self-knowledge and a corresponding reliance on the grace of God. This relationship lasted throughout one's life; not even the death of the elder severed it. Because of the charismatic nature of the relationship,[11] however, the roles could be reversed if the neophyte surpassed the spiritual maturity of the elder.[12]

This relationship with the elder took place within a way of life that both honored the role and the importance of the elder, but that also limited it. In the desert, God was always the first teacher. The cell was the second, and, within the cell, the guidance of the scriptures was the third.[13] Thus, the *abba* or *amma* was the fourth teacher, who helped with discernment and protected the neophyte against self-deception, self-will, and other evasions that prevented the reception of one's unique gift of God. The "words" spoken and the advice given in this form of direction were always particular and concrete, and were intended only for the person addressed. However, although the teachings or instructions given by the elder were deeply personal and applicable only for someone in an analogous situation, the desert dwellers recognized their wisdom and collected the stories and aphorisms, using them as "teaching stories" detached from their original situation. The following is one example of such a story of spiritual direction:

> Abba Anthony's feelings were hurt by another brother and he went to his elder, Abba Sisois. Abba Anthony said: "I want to avenge myself on a brother who hurt me." Abba Sisois replied, "Don't, my son: leave vengeance in the hands of God." Abba Anthony said to Abba Sisois, "I cannot rest until I take revenge." Abba Sisois then stood. "My brother, let us pray. O God, we have no further need to think of you, for we take vengeance ourselves." Abba Anthony in response knelt before Abba Sisois and said, "No longer will I quarrel with my brother: I beg you to forgive me."[14]

This reported story of an encounter with an elder displays the main features of the process: the disclosure of the obsessional feeling bothering the one seeking help, and the elder's ability to shift this negative consciousness by revealing Abba Anthony's state of soul in his prayer.

This model constituted the most individualized form of spiritual direction in the tradition, as it preceded general accounts of spiritual development that affected the practice in later periods. At this stage, it remained completely distinct from the confessor/penitent model. While it placed a high value on the obedience and docility of the younger person in relationship to the *abba* or *amma*, the purpose was to free the younger person of willfulness. One became a guide only on the basis of personal experience and the gift of discernment, and willingly released the other from guidance when its purpose had been achieved. Above all, the compassionate understanding of the human heart was the most highly prized quality in an elder.[15]

The Benedictine Monastic Model

The Benedictine monastic model of spiritual direction included many features of the desert tradition while also incorporating some innovations.[16] Although Benedict used the ideal of the "spiritual father" rooted in the desert tradition as his primary model for the abbot of a stable community, he envisioned a dramatically different context. The monastery was a school, a place of training, meant to lead others to salvation through the practice of the ascetic life.

The Rule itself and community life became the primary form of guidance. The Rule carefully spelled out the external details of life, as well as the desired internal dispositions of heart that all should practice; namely, obedience, silence, humility, and fraternal love. All, including the abbot, were obliged first of all to obey the provisions of the Rule. The abbot had the responsibility of guiding the monks according to individual needs and differences and was to be chosen for qualities of spiritual leadership, especially "discretion."[17] No longer a purely charismatic figure around whom others gathered, the abbot became an officeholder charged with an obligation to teach and direct his community. Although the Rule encouraged a form of individual guidance through manifestation of conscience to the abbot,[18] in practice he often directed his teaching to the community as a whole.

In addition to the abbot, other experienced monks (*seniores*) also served as "spiritual fathers."[19] The novice director passed on a whole way of life by being a personal example, by reading and explaining the Rule, and by discerning the candidates' suitability for the life. William of St. Thierry, an early Cistercian, emphasized the role of the elder in relationship to a novice. The novice entrusted himself totally to the novice director to be formed in God in the feelings and the spirit of humility because he himself lacked discretion and the ability to be discerning in his own case.[20] However, the mature members of the community were also encouraged to practice fraternal obedience to a guide because "in such matters the eye of someone else often has a clearer view of us than our own. Someone else, someone whose will is not prey to the same fervor, is often a better judge of our acts than we are. For often either through negligence or through self-love we have a mistaken idea of ourselves."[21] In addition to this assistance with discernment, one of the seniors also provided support in the spiritual life and shared knowledge of God derived from personal contemplative experience.[22]

In this model of spiritual direction, a trend toward institutionalizing the essential characteristics of the earlier model appeared alongside the charismatic element. Caring for the individual, discerning, and receiving the manifestation of heart from the directee continued; however, these functions might be dispersed among an experienced monastic, an appointed novice director, and the abbot. These persons undertook such roles on the basis of a charism recognized by members of the community. This spiritual-direction relationship existed in the context of an external rule of life and a stable community, which contextualized the role of the guide. The relationship to the elder, originally distinct from the confessor/penitent relationship, gradually began to merge with the practice of sacramental confession. Indeed, with the establishment of the practice of confession in the universal church, frequent "devotional" confession became common for people seeking holiness of life, which linked spiritual direction to the confessional until the contemporary period.[23] Obedience to the Rule, to the abbot, and to the spiritual director continued as a valued method of tempering self-will. All of these relationships were further affected by a communal life of fraternal charity.

A similar model of spiritual direction existed in women's monasteries. The abbess functioned as a spiritual director for her nuns, as did other women in the community. During some parts of the Middle Ages, abbesses held jurisdiction over the male clerics who served the community in a liturgical capacity.[24] With the practice of more frequent confession and the increasing clericalism in the church, however, women, abbesses included, were to a certain extent eventually subject to the direction of male, cleric confessors. Within this model, the story told in spiritual direction was affected by the specific roles each director held in the monastery, as well as by the role of the confessor. What a sister might share with a novice director or abbess could differ remarkably from what she might share with another trusted member of the community.

Late-Medieval Non-Monastic Model

Although the Benedictine/Cistercian monastic model of spiritual direction dominated the Middle Ages, new developments in lay spirituality began to emerge in the twelfth to fifteenth centuries. The Dominican Order (founded in 1216 by Dominic Guzman) was characterized by its concern "to be useful to the souls of our neighbors" and initiated a "third order" group for lay members.[25] The Franciscans (founded ca. 1221 by Francis Bernadone) began as a mendicant lay group, espousing poverty of life and preaching the gospel. Simultaneously, in northern France, Flanders, and Holland, new forms of the *vita apostolica*, characterized by poverty of life and preaching the gospel, emerged in the form of Beguine communities.[26]

Historian Francois Vandenbroucke describes the non-clerical, non-monastic forms of spiritual direction resulting from these new forms of evangelical life as "extra-hierarchical and charismatic."[27] A number of holy women, *mulieres religiosae*,[28] were recognized spiritual directors. Often mystics and frequently ecstatics,[29] they included Hadewijch of Antwerp (writings date ca. 1220–40), Catherine of Siena (1347–80), Julian of Norwich (1343–1416), and Catherine of Genoa (1447–1510).

Hadewijch, who led a Beguine community, was responsible for the spiritual formation of her companions. Her letters, such as Letter 15, testify to her role as spiritual guide: "…and closely observe, with regard either to myself or others in whom you seek sincere practice of virtue, who they are that help you to improve, and consider what their life is. For there are all too few on earth today in whom you can find true fidelity; for almost all people now want from God and men what pleases them and what they desire or lack."[30] Hadewijch had a stormy career, as her community eventually rejected her. She probably wrote the letters both while still a member of the community as well as after she left it.

Laity often consulted Julian of Norwich, a recluse known as a person of good counsel. *The Book of Margery Kempe* provides a contemporary witness to Julian's role as spiritual guide and describes Margery's experience consulting with Julian in considerable detail. Margery claims that she asked Julian's advice about the special grace God had accorded her, "for the ankres was expert in swech thyngys and good cownsel cowd geuyn." She reports Julian's balanced advice and describes the consultation in glowing terms: "Much was the holy dalliance that the anchoress and this creature had by communing in the love of our Lord Jesus Christ on the many days they were together."[31] Although a visionary, Julian exhibited a markedly lesser degree of ecstatic phenomena than did other women, such as those discussed below.

Catherine of Siena and Catherine of Genoa were both laywomen. Catherine of Siena became a member of the *Mantellate*, a Dominican tertiary group, and continued to live at home.

Catherine of Genoa, although she wanted to become a nun at thirteen, agreed to a political marriage arranged by her family. Unhappily married for ten years, she underwent a mystical conversion. Thereafter, she, with her husband's agreement, gave herself to the care of the sick as a nurse and director at the Pannetone Hospital.

The two Catherines attracted groups of disciples, including both clerics and laity. These saintly women engaged in spiritual conversations with their disciples, forming their spirituality and inspiring their active charity. Catherine of Siena called her followers her "family" of which she was their acknowledged "mamma," regardless of the age differences among them. She also dictated numerous letters of spiritual direction and had a remarkable prophetic gift that enabled her to "read other people's secret thoughts and intentions."[32]

All four women wrote or dictated major spiritual writings that derived from their mature mystical development and their encounters with others.[33] They developed their own mystical theology from their experience, in concert with the tradition they had received. Because of their experience in the spiritual life, others sought out these women for instruction, encouragement in faith, and group and individual counsel. Hadewijch and the Catherines gave spiritual direction to the communities gathered around them and eloquently and profoundly communicated their spiritual teaching through their writing, which they produced toward the end of their lives. Some extended their spiritual influence through their male disciples, a common model that included a number of other such women.[34]

Since these holy people were essentially spiritual teachers, their followers asked questions and sought counsel. The response was often a teaching or advice, although visionaries might share the symbols and words received in a vision related to the person seeking counsel.

Ignatian Interventionist Model

Ignatius of Loyola (1495–1556), through the development of the Spiritual Exercises, inaugurated a new interventionist model of spiritual direction. Ignatius developed the text of *The Spiritual Exercises*, a handbook for the one who gives the Exercises, based on experimental self-observation and experience in guiding others through this sequence of active, ascetical exercises.[35] These processes were designed to prepare and dispose "the soul to rid itself of all inordinate attachments, and, after their removal, of seeking and finding the will of God in the disposition of our life for the salvation of our soul."[36] Ignatius described the director specifically as "one who gives the Exercises," usually in an enclosed setting over the course of thirty days.[37] He and his followers later amplified this text with additional commentary called *The Directory of the Exercises*.[38]

In this model, the director, having personal experience as an exercitant,[39] decides who is suitable to engage in this process[40] and determines the manner of prayer and the subject of meditations, examinations of conscience, and imaginative contemplations.[41] The director discerns the meaning, source, and direction of the retreatant's affectivity, commonly referred to as "spirits," and gives instruction on the rules for discernment of spirits as needed.[42] Finally, the director adapts the Exercises to each person.[43] In this active role, the director offers the retreatant the processes and subject matter designed to initiate a particular dynamic. Its purpose is ordering the life and affections of the retreatant in such a way as to dispose him or her to encounter God directly and respond to the divine initiative. After initiating these interventions, the director assumes a background role in order to encourage the retreatant to discover personal meaning from the meditations and to experience and savor intimate experience of God.[44] Ignatius describes this stabilizing role of the retreat director as providing the balance point on a scale.

Those who make the Exercises must be prepared to answer the director's questions about all experiences relevant to the retreat. This requires great generosity of heart and deep trust in the director on the part of the retreatant. Without necessarily knowing the actual sins of the retreatant, the director is to be "kept faithfully informed about the various disturbances and thoughts caused by the action of different spirits,"[45] as well as the graces and fruit of each prayer period. Because the retreatant does not necessarily know the sequence or structure of the Exercises, the director needs to receive the retreatant's account of his or her experience in order to guide the person through the process. The retreatant tells this story of grace and resistance in the process of making the Exercises.

This model of direction had an enormous impact on Counter-Reformation piety in the post-Tridentine church. It proved adaptable to all devout people with sufficient leisure to make the enclosed retreat. It was independent of a monastic lifestyle, its purpose being the formation of people who would actively serve others. The proliferation of printed material, the spread of education through the Jesuit college system, and an adaptation of this model of direction to the confessional helped spread its influence.

Ignatius expected the direction of the Exercises to be individualized in a one-to-one relationship formed solely for the purposes of giving the Exercises. By the seventeenth and eighteenth centuries, however, the content of the Exercises had been adapted to group retreats, the formation of sodalities, and the preaching of missions. This model of direction became a common feature of confessional practice, no longer restricted to the special circumstances of the enclosed retreat.[46] In the contemporary period, the Spiritual Exercises were restored to their individualized form, attracting once again people from all walks of life to engage in this transformative process.[47]

Post-Tridentine Director of Conscience

This model dominated the Catholic tradition for three hundred years after the Council of Trent (1545–63)[48] established the confessor-penitent relationship as the ordinary form of spiritual direction. Indeed, according to the Tridentine definition of penance, the confessor assumed the role of judge and became a superior for those penitents not under the authority of a religious superior.[49]

During this lengthy period, spiritual direction became preoccupied with sin and "cases of conscience"; not surprisingly, scrupulosity emerged as a frequent spiritual problem and theme because the required story was an account of one's sin. This situation implied the need for a specialist with appropriate theological and spiritual training to provide professional solutions for special situations and problems;[50] thus, this model of direction focused on decisions about specialized religious vocations and the directee's progress in mental prayer. In addition, directors viewed themselves as guardians of orthodoxy and teachers of "safe" methods in the face of threats posed by the Protestant Reformation and various mystical movements, such as quietism, illuminism, and Jansenism. Helping their directees avoid heresy and dubious forms of mysticism became a major aspect of their role.[51] Contemplative nuns were required to give an account of their mystical experiences, which were not infrequently received by skeptical guardians of orthodoxy. All these factors led to a more institutionalized type of spiritual direction governed by the rubrics of sacramental confession. The required story of a person seeking spiritual direction was their "sin story," and only after that narrative was completed was the story of vocation or mystical graces welcomed.

The view of God's mediation of grace as well as its general theological context was hierarchical in this model.[52] As a result, it tended to emphasize obedience to the spiritual director. The director/directee relationship clearly lacked mutuality, as the images applied to it show: physician/patient, father/child, superior/subject, confessor/penitent, and, from Francis de Sales, guiding "angel, not merely a man."[53] Similarly, the terms *spiritual direction, spiritual director*, and *directee*, which originate in this historical period, carry connotations of overbearing authority and potentially infantilizing obedience. Although a number of very good and saintly spiritual directors greatly helped holy people during this time, the inherent authoritarianism of the model and the ideology accompanying it frequently resulted in autocratic, incompetent, mediocre, and even ignorant directors exercising tyrannical control over their directees. As early as the sixteenth and seventeenth centuries, prominent voices, including John of the Cross (1542–91), Teresa of Avila (1515–82), and Dom Augustine Baker (1575–1641),[54] complained about the harm such directors did to their directees.

By the early twentieth century, people generally understood spiritual direction as the application of "principles and general rules to each person in particular."[55] One acquired these principles and rules through the study of a systematic treatise on the spiritual life—reading the great masters of the spiritual life (usually from the sixteenth century to the present)—and the "practice of Christian and priestly virtues under the care of a wise director."[56] Although some acknowledged the need for a spiritual director to have personal experience in the spiritual life, spiritual direction for all practical purposes was no longer considered to be a charism. The link with sacramental confession resulted in spiritual direction becoming a function of office and the responsibility of cleric-confessors.

Furthermore, the distortion of the place of spiritual direction in Christian life (required for holiness, yet completely institutionalized) resulted in the adoption of peculiar metaphors to describe the relationship of God, the director, and the person seeking direction to justify the decision not to participate. For example, some spoke of a book or a rule of life taking the place of spiritual direction,[57] and Thérèse of Lisieux wrote of Jesus as "the Director of directors."[58] Descriptions such as these reflect the persistent temptation in this institutionalized form of spiritual direction for the director to assume inappropriate authority over directees.

The fusion of spiritual direction with the confessional did result in making spiritual direction available to all Christians, regardless of their particular vocations, provided they found a suitable director/confessor. Members of recognized religious orders were required by canon law to present themselves to confessors on a weekly basis, as well as to different confessors quarterly. Nonetheless, within such orders, novice directors and superiors also performed many functions of spiritual direction, although matters of conscience remained restricted to the confessional. Many laypersons adopted the practice of frequent confession in order to benefit from spiritual direction.

This post-Tridentine model of spiritual direction was deeply clerical and sexist in its assumptions. The directors applied principles and rules to another's life. Although they derived some principles from experience, they tended to draw their conclusions deductively from the principles. The concrete experience of the person seeking direction had little value and was not necessarily taken into account in the formulation of these principles and rules. This was particularly true of women's experience. The literature of the period betrays an extreme distrust and devaluation of women in the rules and admonitions developed for common use by clerical directors. They implied that women were untrustworthy, susceptible to illusions, and incapable of mature development in the spiritual life.[59] Women were consequently subjected to ecclesiastical male authority to validate their religious experiences and to approve or confirm the authenticity of their writings without having access to the same theological education or training. Under these circumstances, and given the delicacy of the spiritual-direction relationship that requires self-disclosure and trust, women either engaged in this process with men conditioned to be prejudiced against them or only superficially participated in spiritual direction.[60]

Vatican II Contemporary Model

The contemporary model of spiritual direction contrasts remarkably to the previous authoritarian and sacramental one. It has evolved in the ecclesial and cultural context of the Second Vatican Council. While the post-Tridentine model was particularly uncongenial to the Reformation churches and restricted the scope and focus of spiritual direction to Roman Catholicism, the contemporary model is largely once again charismatic and noninstitutional. As in some earlier models, spiritual direction has become distinct from the sacrament of penance. People freely choose a spiritual director of either sex, who may or may not share the same Christian vocation or denomination. Directors are usually expected to be knowledgeable in the spiritual tradition, to understand the dynamics of spiritual development and prayer from personal experience, and to be able to assist with discernment. In this era of psychological self-consciousness, directors are also expected to be conversant with major psychological theories and concepts, especially developmental psychology.

Despite a necessary asymmetry in the relationship, both persons prefer to view each other as mutually growing in the spiritual life and related to each other as peers in Christ. One person assumes a reflecting/listening role in relation to the other only in spiritual-direction sessions. Unlike the monastic model, in the contemporary model, directors and directees do not ordinarily live with each other nor relate to one another outside the direction relationship. Religious orders and seminaries frequently distinguish spiritual direction from formation interviews, which have the goals of passing on a way of life within a particular community or of judging a candidate's suitability for priesthood or a particular form of religious life. Personnel institutionally charged with supervising the formation of new members generally do not also assume the role of spiritual director. Seminarians and candidates are left free to choose a spiritual director outside the formation house.

In the contemporary model, the understanding of authority and obedience has changed. The contemporary belief that others—peers and subordinates, as well as those in authority—can mediate God's will and grace to an individual modifies the former belief that God speaks primarily and most reliably through persons in authority. Obedience consists in the ability to discern God's presence and activity through various possible mediations and to act on that judgment. Contemporary spiritual directors respect the directee's freedom of conscience and responsibility for personal choices. A director, conscious of the psychological dynamic of transference, resists a directee's attempt to avoid personal responsibility for choices by getting the director to tell him or her what to do. Obedience consists in listening to and trying to recognize God's claim in a concrete situation and acting on that judgment accordingly. The director's authority resides in the truth of an insight that emerges from the shared exploration of a situation or from greater personal experience or knowledge than the directee. The focus on obedience shifts from valuing obedience for its own sake, without reference to the merits of what is commanded, to the cultivation of discerning hearts. Thus, discernment in relationship to the concrete situations that confront a person becomes central to spiritual direction.

The director's role is understood as genuinely helpful yet auxiliary. God's action is primary and necessary. Spiritual directors describe themselves as co-discerners, listeners, companions, midwives, soul-friends, and spiritual companions. We acknowledge that God, or the Holy Spirit, is the guide or director for each person. The spiritual director's role involves helping the other recognize and respond to the divine direction.[61] This approach encourages directees to tell their sacred tales of grace and struggle, mystery and wonder, ministry and relationships. Discernment results from reflection on these stories of interior movements: experiences of transcendence and experiences of graced activity.

Instead of applying principles or rules to individual cases, the contemporary model of spiritual direction concerns itself with the concrete religious experience of the individual. Influenced by a theology of the human person—which takes embodiment, history, social context, and process seriously—and by a theory of knowledge that moves from the concrete and particular to the general and abstract, contemporary spiritual directors value the particular and unique experiences of their directees in a quite different way than did those in previous periods.

It is important to note that each of the previous historical models of spiritual direction continues in an adapted form in some contexts in the present era. The desert *amma* or *abba* has not entirely disappeared and may be found today in the Egyptian desert where that form of monasticism is enjoying a renaissance. Likewise, the Russian or Eastern Orthodox *starets* is more in continuity with this model than with the contemporary Western model described above. The Ignatian model continues to focus on guiding another through the process of the *Spiritual Exercises*, and reference to the dynamics of the Exercises remains a touchstone in all Ignatian spiritual direction, whether or not a directee is actually making the Exercises at a given time. And in the tension between Vatican II–renewal and restorationist tendencies among some segments of the Roman Catholic Church, the post-Tridentine authoritarian director has not disappeared. Spiritual directors in various Protestant traditions have largely adopted the contemporary model and often adapt it to their communities. For instance, directors in the Reformation traditions will emphasize the role of scripture more than perhaps those from sacramental traditions.

The Problem of Terminology

Language about spiritual direction immediately elicits feelings based on the image or model of direction evoked. Spiritual directors have yet to resolve the problems created by language rooted in some models. The classic terminology for spiritual direction is not altogether satisfactory. Spiritual paternity or maternity is insufficiently egalitarian for many and seems to apply to a rather limited number of actual spiritual-direction relationships. Some people prefer to use a friendship model for spiritual direction. Although a fully mutual spiritual friendship may occur with some people, this does not seem to be the case for the majority. Furthermore, gifted spiritual directors who meet with many directees cannot possibly enter into each relationship in a fully mutual way. Despite its appeal, the language of spiritual friendship or soul-friend neither differentiates the roles in spiritual direction nor accounts for the actual asymmetry in the relationship. It may also be responsible for some spiritual directors' failing to assume responsibility for the directee's safety.

Many people do not find the language of the clerical model of *confessor/penitent*, nor the medical model of *doctor/patient*, nor the psychiatric model of *therapist/client* helpful in describing the direction relationship. Likewise, others dislike the authoritarian overtones of *director/directee* language. Some have replaced these terms with *guide* and *guided*. Nevertheless, many continue to use *director/directee* terminology because it distinguishes the respective roles in the relationship, allows us to relate the contemporary experience of spiritual direction to the tradition, and can be redefined in acceptable ways.[62]

Assumptions about Spiritual Direction

Spiritual direction is currently enjoying a renaissance, which began shortly after Vatican II for Roman Catholics, and which shows no sign of waning as it expands to other Christian denominations and other religions.[63] Because of the rapid pace of change in our contemporary experience, more and more people are seeking spiritual direction as an important spiritual practice. This continuing growth of the ministry is responsible for a growing body of literature about spiritual direction.[64]

Although the purpose of spiritual direction has remained constant (the growth in the spiritual life of the person seeking direction), the conception of it has changed throughout history. My approach to spiritual direction focuses on the narrative aspects of these conversations and relies on the following assumptions about spiritual direction:

1. It has as its purpose the spiritual growth of the person seeking direction.

2. Two Christians engage with one another in an ongoing relationship for this purpose. The practice of interfaith spiritual direction is currently growing and changes the narrative horizons of the participants.

3. The conversations focus on the experienced interaction of God with the person seeking direction and that person's response to these movements both within prayer and in daily life.

4. Both persons participate in discernment; that is, in discriminating how God seems to be leading the person toward action or response.

5. Although both persons are fallible Christians trying to follow God's call within the context of Christian faith and community, the person serving as guide or director has some capacity to help the other by virtue of the depth of personal graced experience, the gift of discernment, experience with self and others, and sufficient knowledge of the spiritual tradition and ordinary human development.

6. Because direction focuses on spiritual growth, the spiritual-direction encounter presupposes that the person seeking direction consciously relates to God, however mysteriously or vaguely named.

7. This experienced relationship (or its possibility) to a transcendent Other places the conversation within the sphere of divine influence for both persons. God leads, directs, guides.[65]

Narrative in Spiritual Direction

This reflection on the narrative and interpretive dimensions of spiritual direction is an invitation to both beginning and experienced spiritual directors to deepen their understanding of the spiritual-direction process as a storytelling, story-listening situation and to become more skillful in responding to their directees' stories.

Since I began in the field a quarter-century ago, my conviction about the importance of storying in the spiritual-direction process has only deepened and expanded. First, the international students whom I have mentored as a supervisor immediately embrace an oral style of storytelling. Many come from predominately oral cultures that rely on proverbs and stories to pass on their traditional wisdom. Most teaching and learning occur in the context of shared storytelling. Storytelling is a universal human activity. These spiritual-direction interns grasp the process of spiritual direction more easily through story than through psychological theories that they eventually learn to assimilate and appreciate.

Second, for those directees most affected by the cultural shift known as postmodernism, telling one's sacred story in spiritual direction or another pastoral context helps to overcome the fragmentation of identity and the erosion of meaning that often results from encountering conflicting viewpoints and the relativization of religious traditions and their "master narratives." It is almost as if the influence of postmodernism intensifies the need to order experience and to discover meaning through personal narrative.[66] Third, a focus on the way a directee's story unfolds helps beginning directors to connect one session to another, to notice patterns and unfolding plots, and to use their skills of exploring and reflecting feelings in a larger context of life and meaning.

This book explores the implications of identifying the directee's speech as a story and analyzes it in narrative categories.[67] Whatever else spiritual direction involves, it is fundamentally a narrative activity. In rare cases, gifted spiritual directors read people's hearts without their verbal self-disclosure, but most directors depend on the verbal and nonverbal discourse of the person seeking direction. Frequently, and in my experience characteristically, the directee offers a narrative. Insofar as we try to understand and respond to what the person seeking direction says, we also engage in a hermeneutical process; that is, understanding and interpreting that narrative together with the directee. In subsequent chapters, we will explore why people elaborate narratives in the contemporary context of spiritual direction, notice the effects of this storytelling for both the director and directee, identify and describe the distinctive features of these narratives, and discuss some of the implications of this narrative approach for the practice of spiritual direction.

Questions for Further Reflection

1. Does this historical survey of spiritual direction illuminate any of your experiences in spiritual direction?

2. Do you agree or disagree with any of these assumptions about the contemporary model of spiritual direction?

3. How does each model of spiritual direction influence the story the directee tells in spiritual direction?

4. What difference does it make for a directee to be required to tell his or her "sin" story before a "grace" story?

Chapter One
Two Stories of Spiritual Direction[1]

Sam's Experience of Spiritual Direction

Sam was a gay man who belonged to a religious order. (He entered religious life prior to subsequent Vatican guidelines regarding the admission of homosexuals to the priesthood.) Having already completed the novitiate, he wrote his narrative of spiritual direction near the end of his formation and ministerial training leading to priestly ordination. He was in the second year of a three-year master of divinity degree program and lived in a small group with several other members of his community. This group related to the larger religious community working or studying in the academic community and was affected by decisions made by the rector and his staff.

Because Sam was simultaneously engaged in psychotherapy, his spiritual-direction sessions included much less psychological content and an almost exclusive focus on prayer and his spiritual life than is frequently the case with others. Additionally, because of his experience with telling a Freudian story in therapy to reinterpret his childhood experiences, Sam very clearly understood how his experience in spiritual direction resulted in a story different from the one he was telling in therapy. The differences were not so much conflicting interpretations of experience, but rather in spiritual direction he told portions of his therapy story and other experiences within the context of faith and religious experience.

Sam's Story

I am a thirty-year-old member of a religious community; I am currently studying theology and will be ordained a priest in June. During my time in religious life, I have had ongoing spiritual direction of varying quality. My previous director was transferred from Berkeley, and a year ago I began work with my present director. We had been in one class together, and she had done some work with my previous director, so she was not a total stranger to me. I chose to work with her because of good, personal impressions; as I thought about working with her, the idea of working with a woman grew more appealing. I had never done spiritual direction with a woman before, and as I was planning to begin psychotherapy with a man, I thought the balance of male and female input would be helpful.

The academic year that this case study covers was one of intense personal and spiritual deepening. The previous year had been a very difficult one due to a confluence of a number of personal issues. As I began my work with this director, I was aware of a need for healing, for integration of those personal issues, and for some sort of decision regarding my application for ordained ministry. Soon after beginning spiritual direction, I began psychotherapy. Then and now, I felt the processes to be related, but dealing with different issues in my personal identity. Spiritual direction consisted of meetings every other week for approximately one and one-half hours. During that time, our conversations covered a number of topics.

This case study presents the year in such a way as to give a sense of the period's ongoing dynamic. Within that narrative, I will focus on three overlapping topics: prayer and religious experience, discernment, and, for lack of a better word, "moments of insight."

I have a clear memory of our first meeting in early September. My way of presentation in a significant interview is to throw "bait on the waters," so to speak. I begin very generally, filling out nothing of the story. I get a sense of how the person is going to respond, and if that sense is positive, he/she has my trust. I tend to be honest and revelatory rather quickly, once I trust the other. I was true to form in that meeting. After some small talk, I gave a very brief and vague sketch of my life, leaving out significant details. She listened, and then said, "Would you like to tell me a little more about those issues?" I remember very quickly that I was not threatened by the question. I intuitively sensed that the director was trustworthy, and decided to tell much of my story then and there—a disastrous and difficult previous year, my struggles in coming to grips with some aspects of my identity, my decision to begin psychotherapy, my moving to a new community, the problems in my family. I surprise myself with my honesty in such initial situations, and I think my director was somewhat surprised in this one.

The conversation moved to prayer, which I described, in a somewhat embarrassed way, as not well focused, having consistency but little else. She then encouraged me to describe my praying, what I actually did in prayer. I used the phrase "yakking with God"—walking in the neighborhood and talking familiarly with the Lord. The director affirmed my way of prayer; she used the phrase "yakking with God" positively, and, while encouraging me "to be quiet once in a while so that it's a conversation, not a monologue," affirmed my style of prayer. No one had ever done that for me. I was appreciative and told her so. We talked a little then about introverted and extraverted prayer—mine is clearly the latter—the validity of different styles, and the possibility of "being silent in movement." This was wonderful for me; I confessed that I had never found yoga postures helpful. All of this was the first conversation about my prayer style that I had ever had. It was a breakthrough experience for me, which cemented my trust of the director.

As can be seen, my understanding of prayer was rather limited and limiting. I also tended to ignore any "God experience" that did not fit those limits and to downgrade experiences that I could explain away or psychologize. One such experience occurred early in October:

Sam: I want to tell you about something that happened. I really lost it.

June: Tell me what happened.

Sam: Well, I was at the diaconate ordination, and I usually get weepy-eyed at those things to begin with. But once the rite of ordination started, I lost it. I just started crying, especially as the names of people I knew well were called. I cried for about twenty minutes. In fact, W, who was sitting next to me, held my head to his chest, I was crying so hard. And I couldn't stop, and people were looking at me...

June: What were you feeling as this was happening?

Sam: I felt an overwhelming acceptance by God. In spite of my own doubts about ordination and all, I had the feeling that I was accepted just the way I am—that if there are any problems, they are mine, not God's.

June: Do you realize what happens when you describe that experience as "losing it"... that you are giving priority to the embarrassment rather than the presence of God? I don't think you lost it. God touched you in a very powerful and personal way.

I understood her point, and that helped to transform the experience into a touchstone of God's presence over the year. I am a slow learner, though.

About a month later, I was sheepishly describing an experience of tears and God's presence that I had while listening to a contemporary song—"I Need You," by the Pointer Sisters. I remember introducing the experience to her by saying, "This is kind of corny..."

June: Experience of God is not "corny." By describing it that way, you are lessening the power of the experience. Let the experience be what it is.

Sam: I understand what you are saying.

My tendency to slight my experience of God has at least part of its source in a fear of getting too involved with God. I suspect I am afraid of what might happen if I take it all at face value.

Another event of tying my relationship closer to God occurred in March. At that time I spoke about experiencing great sadness and pain regarding my family.

June: As you are talking, I can't help but think of Jesus' agony in the garden. What you are describing is your own experience of that. Perhaps you can let that become part of your prayer… to let the Lord give you a way to express what you don't have words for.

Sam: You know, I've been thinking about that scene for some reason, but I'd never made the connection…

I *did* make the connection, and it has given me a lasting insight on how to incorporate the Jesus story into my own.

In addition to focusing on experiences of God, our spiritual-direction conversations frequently dealt with experiences of living in a small community and of relationships with individuals. Autumn was a good time for me. Academically, I was in a challenging semester that was going well. My new community was turning out wonderfully. We were a group of eight, many of whom had also had difficult experiences the previous year, and we meshed well.

We chose to deal, as a community, with a member of our house whose alcohol consumption was a concern to us. This was a confrontational situation in which I played a strongly supportive role. I found myself amazed that a community could respond to conflict positively and was equally amazed that people respected what I said. In direction, we discussed the dynamics of all of this, especially regarding the process of the alcohol intervention. As the son of a deceased alcoholic father, I was particularly sensitive to and affected by a person showing signs of alcoholic behavior. Direction helped me clarify my own needs and expectations in this situation. Eventually, my relationship with this man became very rewarding.

Two other relationships became important. One was with someone I had lived with the previous year and with whom I had not gotten along. Much healing was brought to that relationship. The other is a relationship that continues to be significant for me. In October, I began going out to lunch once a month with another member of my living group. This relationship has become a solid friendship.

In addition to beginning a new spiritual-direction relationship, I initiated therapy in a classic psychoanalytic mode. This experience was both difficult and rewarding. As I described above, I tend to reveal myself full force when comfortable. Consequently, therapy moved through issues with rapidity. As the therapeutic relationship became a regular one, my focus in spiritual direction moved to another dominant issue—ordination.

Over the year, I suppose there were a number of small discernments, but I think they were all related to my decision to apply for ordination to the priesthood. My letter of petition needed to be written by the end of January. This topic was part of the direction conversation from October on, and it took center stage between Thanksgiving and the middle of January. I had many issues around it. The first to deal with was my freedom to apply, which demanded also the freedom not to apply. We dealt with this soon after I spent an evening with my mother in the middle of October.

Sam: I feel as though she's got [my ordination] all planned out...She's really looking forward to it...and I understand it.

June: But you don't have the freedom to say no...

| **Sam:** | I can say no if I want, but I don't know what I want yet. |
| **June:** | Maybe telling your mother that you don't know will give you the space you need in which to decide. |

As a matter of fact, it did. Telling my mother took the pressure off the decision, and allowed me to deal with the next issue: readiness. I felt that I was not ready to be ordained. I had not really clarified this when I spoke about it in direction. I remember saying that I "didn't have my act together yet." We explored some causes of that feeling—being in therapy, moving communities, etc. Going through the causes, I realized that they weren't the issue. The key was to realize, as I did in direction, that I would never be "ready," that God uses me *as I am* for ministry. It is God doing the work, not my "act" that is or isn't together.

From unreadiness arose feelings of unworthiness. In one session, I told how I had this vague feeling of not being good enough.

June:	If it's okay with you, I'd like you to try and visualize this feeling.
Sam:	I'm game.
June:	Close your eyes... relax... let yourself picture this force... When you can, describe it to me.
Sam:	(some silence) It's a man, or boy, smaller than me... It's wooden... just standing there, trying to scare me with a roar, but he's just a small puppet... It's Pinocchio! (laughter)
June:	(with somewhat of a mocking scowl) Not so powerful after all.

I remember feeling foolish, but also sure that worthiness was not the issue. That revealed itself in the conversation that followed:

June: What else are you uneasy about in all this?

Sam: Well, all of my work in therapy is making me wonder about my attitudes toward family life.

June: Tell me a bit more about this.

Sam: I knew I had a problem with my Dad because of his drinking and erratic behavior at home. But now, I'm getting in touch with very painful feelings about my Mom. Our family life was really pretty difficult, you know.

June: Is it possible that you chose priestly life partly because your experience of family life was so conflictual and confusing?

Sam: Well, being gay is not the easiest thing in the church. I still have my own uneasiness with my gay identity, and I wonder how I will fit into the church with its attitudes, and what will happen in the future.

June: Hold on a minute… What do you feel about your being a gay man?

Sam: I am accepted in my community… Everyone knows who needs to know… but if I weren't doing this… You know, Castro Street² is a nice place to visit, but that's not me. It really isn't…

June: You don't seem to have a reasonable alternative for yourself. Religious life versus Castro Street is not a real choice for you… It's impossible to make a free choice if there isn't a real option. Can you imagine what you would want if you weren't a religious?

Sam: (pause) I would be in a stable relationship with a lover. I'd be teaching high school somewhere, and we'd be close to San Francisco, and have a yard that I could work in…(another pause)… I

> have to think about that... That's a real choice
> for me...

That prayer encounter was pretty powerful. I found I could imagine a healthy life as a gay man with a partner, complete with a garden to work in and a job teaching high school. But when I brought all that to prayer, I felt even more strongly attracted to the priesthood. I prayed over all this and made a decision that had some freedom.

The scene shifts to early February:

Sam: Well, I wrote it.

June: Congratulations! Tell me about it.

Sam: I sat down where I pray and began to write. And I cried. I felt confirmed... and the letter just flowed. I made very few changes for the final draft.

June: Sounds as if the Spirit has been moving with you through the whole process.

The year continued well. Community continued to be wonderful, and I found myself growing rooted in the new house with the people there. I experienced a personality conflict with one member of the community that direction helped me clarify. Therapeutically, ongoing day-to-day material was present, but my main agenda was working out my relationship with my father, one which was far more complex and in which I had had far more power than I realized. Obviously, such insights helped me in day-to-day living as well, but my focus in therapy was on the past. The work was always difficult, at times very difficult. As I went through therapy, the question of ordination was present. At no time did any issues that would have suggested a delay in moving toward ordination present themselves. I felt grounded in that decision even as my whole life was periodically up for reinterpretation.

Into the spring, community issues dominated direction. There was a serious question as to where our community would be living the next year, and direction helped me to separate my personal authority issues from those involving community politics. My director's experience as a woman religious who has been through her own battles was very helpful here. Through talking about the personal and political aspects of decision making about community housing, I got to the point where I could lay this issue aside and not take the whole thing personally.

Lest it seem that only critical conversations occurred in spiritual direction, it is important to say that our sessions also had their noncritical moments, and I think our conversation helped me to gain insight on those as well. Two incidents stand out for me, one in the fall and one in the spring. The earlier one centered around the aforementioned evening with my mother, in which she related some family history that was both convoluted and inappropriate. As I grappled with that, my director suggested I look at my mother's experience as a Catholic woman, married in the early 1950s to an alcoholic man who died and left her a widow.

June: Do you realize that she couldn't talk about the things she told you? She was expected to be quiet and raise a family. What she's talking about are things she couldn't talk about then.

Sam: But why me? And why over dinner?

June: Because somehow, you're safe. She may not realize what she's saying, but she's saying it.

This insight continues to be tremendously helpful as I deal with her. Another type of insight occurred in the spring, again around the extreme sadness and pain I was experiencing regarding my family.

Sam: I feel as though this pain is like an open, running sore, one that just has to ooze and bleed until it dries, and when it heals, it will leave this big scar.

32

June:	Does it have to leave a scar?
Sam:	Huh?
June:	Well, can't healing take place without leaving a scar? Can a wound heal cleanly, leaving only a trace of a scar, or no scar at all?
Sam:	I guess it could. I never thought of that.
June:	The way you think about it will shape the way you heal.

The wound has almost healed, and I don't think the scar will be huge.

As the school year ended, I found myself pleased with the results. Therapy continued to be difficult and profitable. My focus had shifted to my relationship with my mother, and direction was helpful here. The community stayed virtually intact and in the same place, both of which were a relief. My own self-image had shifted as well; I was better able to hear positive comments to me and about me. On a faith-sharing weekend late in April, one of my community members told me that I was one of the most impressive people he had ever lived with. I shared this experience with my director, all the while fumbling as to why it was so significant.

June:	What strikes me is the fact that T, who gave you the compliment, is the one with whom you risked involvement in the alcohol intervention in the fall. In a way, you helped him do something about his drinking, something you couldn't do for your father. Do you see a link there?

I did, and I continue to see many of the links between the conversation of direction and my ongoing story.

I hope the reader has caught the flavor of my experience of direction over the year. I see our conversations as allowing me to retell and reshape my own story, to clarify its meaning, and to give me better insight into its more significant events.

Mary's Experience of Retreat Direction

When Mary wrote her narrative, she was a laywoman enrolled in a degree program to prepare for ministries in retreat work, spiritual direction, and teaching. Her story focuses on an important retreat, describing both her experience of prayer and of retreat direction. Her story of the retreat focuses primarily on her director's accurate perception of her emotional distress caused by her recent divorce. As is often the case in spiritual direction, it is both appropriate and necessary to pay attention to such issues.

Mary's Story[3]

This case is the story of an eight-day directed retreat, which occurred three years ago when I was twenty-eight years old, and two months after my husband left the marriage. I had been happily married for eight years when my husband, after completing an advanced degree, left suddenly by having an affair. This created a crisis for me. I was terrified, experiencing an immense sense of failure and loss. I couldn't believe that this could happen to me. Divorce was something that happened to other people, to people who didn't care about their marriages and hadn't put time into them. In total shock, I went on retreat. This was the third directed retreat I had had with the same spiritual companion with whom I had built up a relationship of trust. This trust was crucial at a time when the man I had trusted most had betrayed me.

Arrival

I arrived at the retreat center feeling numb, yet pleased to be in that place of peace again. My spiritual companion came to meet me, gave me an all-encompassing hug, and said, "Mary, I was shocked to hear your news. I couldn't believe the words in your letter." My eyes just filled with tears. I didn't say anything. He added, "I want you to know, if you need more time to

34

talk, if something comes up at an unscheduled time, just come and find me. I want this time to be as helpful as possible for you." It was life-giving to be so warmly accepted.

Day One

I just spent time settling in, sleeping, and awakening my numb senses to the smells, tastes, and beauty that were surrounding me. I began to slow down, to walk slower and become quieter externally and internally. I explored the sense of touch, absorbing and being saturated with the nature that surrounded me. The garden was beautifully cared for, with colorful, dainty flowers; the grassy areas were wide and inviting while in the distance the mountains reminded me that there were peaks and valleys to climb during my retreat. I contrasted the stone of the buildings with the softness of the grass—all symbolically representing the many and varied emotions I would have at this time. The scripture passage I used that day was "as certain as the dawn he will come." I became certain of God's presence in the whole history of my relationship with him. I longed for that relationship to be more fulfilled.

Day Two

As I came to be quiet before the Lord, my openness and receptivity improved. I became more able to hear the Lord's words to me. I was quite aware of how lost, empty, and rejected I felt but stopped intellectualizing about it and moved into the feelings. A friend had placed a copy of the prayer "Footprints" under my door. I used this as a constant reminder that God was with me.

I expressed to my spiritual companion that I felt I had lost my best friend, my confidant, and my lover, and that all I had left was a profound sense of emptiness. I had an image of myself gradually disintegrating into nothing, dissolving into a thousand tiny pieces that could never be repaired because they were so fragmented and brutally torn. I felt worthless and motionless with no chance of building a new future, no hope that I could ever be happy again. I felt that I had been tried, convicted, and crucified publicly in a most demeaning and humiliating way. I felt like the Christ figure in a paraliturgy I'd done with my class before the retreat. We made Christ a clown with a white face. As he was crucified, someone came and tore his mask into a thousand tiny pieces. I identified with Christ's pain so much. My spiritual companion just listened and cared for me during all of this. He suggested that these feelings were natural, and that I was actually managing very well. We began to talk about B, my husband.

Ralph:	Mary, who married whom? Did B marry you, or did you just want him to marry you?
Mary:	(a shocked pause) Yes, I married B. He didn't marry me.
Ralph:	One person cannot make a marriage, no matter how hard he or she tries. You did the best you could.

This really helped me to begin to deal with the extreme sense of failure I was feeling. My spiritual director added, "Perhaps we may be able to see a glimmer of resurrection during the retreat."

I also talked about the nightmares I had been having, in which I would wake up paralyzed. I was afraid at home in the house. My spiritual companion's response was, "Do you think you could open just one window a little when you go home? It sounds as if you are shutting everyone out of your life."

I was so hurt I was unable to express it to anyone. I would often cry and cry on my own. The only event in Christ's life that could bear the weight of how I felt was the crucifixion. Prayer that day began in tears, darkness, and silence. Then the image of Christ crucified began to take on much the same expression and scars that my shattered face had. I came to know that my pain was his pain and his pain mine. Scars that were bleeding on his face were also bleeding on mine, yet his eyes revealed a great capacity for love and constant hope. In his torn, weeping, and rejected state, he embraced me. I became still and dwelled waiting, for I felt I had nothing else. I began to abandon my own being and really trust in God.

That evening, I had to be honest with myself. The thing I feared most, that I simply didn't want to talk about, was my sexuality; I knew that I had to face this.

> **Mary:** Ralph, what I really need to talk about is my sexuality. I am having a great deal of difficulty expressing in words what I want to say. I keep having a vision of B making love with Y. This breaks my heart. He didn't tell me that this had happened but I knew. I dreamed about it, and when he was home the next morning, I confronted him with this. I went to him to hug him and say it would be all right, but he pushed me away. I kept remembering this rejection and longed for someone to hug me, to touch me, and not to see me as repulsive.

> **Ralph:** Mary, that is a language that you are used to using; it is natural to want to keep using it. That is your language and it is beautiful. I have often found that people whose spouses have died experience similar feelings. They have found it extremely helpful to take these feelings of desertion, emptiness, and longings to prayer. As your body aches for someone to touch you, allow the Lord to do this.

I thought very carefully about this and began to put it into action. I continually used the image of crucifixion. I knew that Jesus was with me. I felt I knew exactly what he felt like: torn, bleeding, and broken in body—but his spirit was strong. His spirit became united with mine. This became life-giving and energizing. I began to feel more peaceful. I took a long walk that day. I ventured out into the countryside for about four miles. I climbed boulders of limestone and found a place where I could look down on a valley of ferns and undergrowth. Earlier I had stayed close to the retreat house. I had gone down into the caves where I'd be covered with overhanging branches. At this point in the retreat, I felt I could look down on the world and get a wider vision. The sun was shining and I felt that I would try to hand over my feelings to God.

Day Three

This day we talked about how things were financially and how I would manage. I had many bills to pay and was very short of money. I hated having to take on this responsibility, but reluctantly had worked out how I could gradually pay off all the bills.

Ralph: You are a very capable person; you could be a leader, but you evade responsibility. You need to develop this now.

I was shocked to hear this. I talked about all the things B did for me and how difficult I found it, now that I had to do everything for myself.

Ralph: That was not good for you to discuss everything with B and then let him make all the decisions. Why haven't you developed the parts of your personality that are like your father?

This really made me stop and think. I had had a difficult relationship with my father and abhorred his aggression. I, in response, had become particularly passive, timid, and nonassertive. I became determined to work on this.

Ralph: Are you angry about what B did to you?

Mary: No, I just love him so much I could never be angry.

Ralph: You have a right to be. He let you down, shattered your hopes and dreams, and you're not angry?

Mary: Well, I'm not. (I had an inability to express my anger.)

Ralph: If you get a chance, tell him how you feel.

Mary: Do you think I should? I thought it better to keep it to myself.

Ralph: No, be assertive about your feelings.

I did a profile of myself that day of the things God liked in me and the things I thought he disliked. I began to see myself as I really was. I became very upset about my sinfulness, yet at the same time I knew that God wished only for my conversion. I experienced how understanding, tolerant, loving, and positive the Lord was and how patient. That evening at the communal reconciliation, I was asked to embrace my friend "Judas," the betrayer of my life. I struggled to name and embrace this all day and was finally happy to hand it over to the Lord that evening. I did this with an undertone of sadness that I could not love as I was loved. After this reconciliation I had an incredible sense of being healed.

Day Four

I felt that I was really opening myself to the Lord and was longing just to be filled with the Lord. I continued to take my feelings of loneliness and longing to prayer. I talked about my opportunity to grieve the loss of B. My spiritual companion suggested that I continue to pray the way I had been, but to put more effort into structuring prayer time.

That evening I was restless, trying to pray. I couldn't and was annoyed with myself. I decided to take a walk through the garden. The stars were out. It was a beautiful, clear autumn evening. Then I had an exchange of love that took me beyond control. I felt as if I were in a mystical garden, fresh and life-giving. I was alone and yet was not alone. I felt surrounded in light and felt weightless. There was an incredible sense of peace. I knew then that there was ultimately only myself and God. At first I felt frightened, but this was very quickly followed by a sense of confidence and freedom. This was all part of the mystery that began to heal me. The insurmountable problems facing me now took on new dimensions; they were still there, but were clothed with new meaning. Eventually I knew that I would have the energy to face them one by one. I came to know that I was loved unconditionally in a way I had not thought possible.

Ralph: How was your day?

Mary: I am praying much better now.

Ralph: Can you describe your prayer to me?

Mary: It's very difficult to put into words.

Ralph: Without saying too much to take away from the preciousness of the experience, could you just say something?

I described the experience of God in the garden. My spiritual companion looked pleased—reverent.

Ralph: I don't know what you did yesterday, but whatever it was, God is confirming your life. Just keep going the way you are with prayer.

Day Five

I had a dream that night that I found particularly significant to all that was happening. A young, shallow girl with a flawless face had been replaced by a scarred, wrinkled woman. The older woman had true beauty; her eyes were sad yet comforting and loving. I could see that she had suffered deeply and during this time had learned what loving really meant. It was then I realized that, if I really loved my husband, I would let him be free, and I would make a new life for

40

myself, a life that would be richer and fuller than it had been previously. In direction, we talked about the possibility that, since my self-image was changing, perhaps my image of God would need to change, too. Ralph suggested that I might like to use more maternal images of God such as those in Isaiah.

This appealed to me as I had been asking myself the crucial question: Would God desert me just as B had? During this retreat God didn't leave me but became ever present, all-loving, and totally understanding. I felt I was being penetrated by God. At the same time, I was tentative. I had a reverence tinged with wonder and fear, yet I was confident that eventually things would become clear.

Day Six

I felt that I was being strengthened to go home and to live more confidently. I knew that God would be with me on that journey. That night, I had a dream of the house being torn apart. I knew that B was taking half the furniture while I was away. Although we had split it fairly, I was worried about what would be gone and how I'd manage. I also had to go back to school and face everyone again.

Mary: I don't know what I am going to do with my life now. Do you think this is God's way of telling me I should join a religious order?

Ralph: (laughed) I don't think that would be a good idea.

Mary: What could I do now? With no one to love, what would I do?

He advised me not to make any decisions while I was in a state of desolation.

Day Seven

During our final interview, my spiritual companion talked about the story of Thomas.

41

Ralph: Think of Thomas. Remember when he asked to put his hands into the wounds of Jesus—that unless he could do this, he could not believe. Remember this as you go home. Thomas was so wise. He knew that in order for Christ to be authentic he needed to have suffered. In order for Thomas to mirror his master, to believe in a way that made their lives one, he too must become part of that suffering to enter it and to experience it.

Mary: I had another dream that seems important. I was in an accident in which my head had come off. When I looked closely, there was still a tiny piece of skin attached. A friend put my head back on and was bandaging me.

Ralph: This is a sign that resurrection has begun. Your head wasn't quite off and the bandages were on.

I identified with Thomas later. This was a great comfort for me in my suffering. I felt I was being refined to become more like Christ. As I went home, I was scared yet hopeful. I felt my emptiness had been filled with the Lord, that I lived not alone but that Christ was in me. I was sober about what I had to face. I lived out of the retreat experience. Six months later, it was still real, and I wrote my annulment papers with help from the retreat.

Conclusion

The retreat initiated the process of gradually reassembling the pieces of my story into a new, creative, and exciting one. I found hope and knew that I wanted to be a lover of life again but a passionate lover. I was no longer someone's wife but an individual. I grew to know myself at my worst and had many of my fears and weaknesses identified. I felt that my spiritual companion had helped mediate God's wish that I be whole again. I began to try to build on my strengths and embrace my weaknesses. I continually reflected on why I hadn't developed the more assertive parts of my personality. I remembered my spiritual companion's words that I was extremely capable and I was not working at my full potential. I began to believe that God was confirming my life—that my life moved God to joy and my suffering moved God to compassion.

Because I had no one to rely on or to make decisions for me, I was forced to face the specific realities of my life and grow up. The retreat was particularly helpful in this regard as it confirmed that I was gradually rebuilding my life story in a positive way. I listened very carefully to the words of advice my director had given me.

The director's responses helped me in the creation of my new story and opened me to the direction of God in my life. The most crucial response he made was in his attentive listening and deep care and concern for my well-being. He created an atmosphere of acceptance, trust, and support yet he encouraged independence. As I shared my story with him, I came to realize the sacredness and uniqueness of these events. I came to know that God was co-creator in the events that unfolded. He was aware of my tone of voice, my body language, and the messages not articulated. His responses helped me see patterns, emotions, and conflicts. He pointed out, in a supportive way, parts of my personality that needed to be developed. He highlighted and brought forward different facets of the narrative and explored them with me, helping me make connections that enabled me to begin to resolve difficulties. His comments and reassurance helped me discern that God was working in my life and gave me guidance on how to be in touch with his presence. He enabled me to grow in self-knowledge by revealing patterns of behavior that were not immediately obvious. When I found it difficult to talk, he listened in such a way that welcomed my efforts. He helped me see God's presence in the ordinary events of my life and to become aware of how I was responding.

Chapter Two
It Takes Two to Discover What Sort of Tale We've Fallen Into

Spiritual-direction narratives emerge within a relational dialogue with a spiritual director. This conversation involves the same type of give and take as any other kind of conversation. The directee—through telling his or her graced story, often in response to the director's questions and responses—interprets his or her life in the light of a concrete experience of God through this process. Hermeneutics is the philosophical name given to such a process of interpretation and understanding. Both the director and the directee necessarily collaborate in seeking greater understanding of the directee's life story and experience of God. Both are engaged in this meaning-making and interpretive process. It takes two to discover the shape of each person's story.

A narrative approach to spiritual direction can be understood more adequately if its dependence on theories of interpretation becomes more explicit. To do so requires drawing on both the philosophical hermeneutics of Hans-Georg Gadamer and the theological hermeneutics of David Tracy. Different understandings about how one can talk about God and the self have been deeply challenged by postmodern theory. It is necessary to ask the question theologian Scott Holland does: "How do stories save us?"[1] Western postmodernism as a worldview has eroded the compelling meaning of any "master narrative," including that of Judeo-Christian religious traditions.

Practicing a religion and consciously relating to the "living God" require a sense of self and of one's religious tradition that continues to name self and God in the context of this more pluralistic way of thinking—because human persons continue to create identities of self and others in and through stories of God, and in and through stories of selves involved with that God and with one another, even if their approach is not the only credible way of doing so. It appears that we live and think through metaphors and narratives as a fundamental given of human experience.

Hans-Georg Gadamer, a German philosopher who pioneered hermeneutical theory in the humanities, uses genuine "conversation" as a model for how persons understand. These conditions apply to spiritual direction that is both a genuine conversation and a process of understanding.

Conditions of a Conversation

As mentioned above, spiritual direction ordinarily takes place in a one-to-one conversational relationship; two people meet at regular intervals to focus on the spiritual life of the person seeking direction and to support that person's growth in the Christian life. In *Truth and Method*, Hans-Georg Gadamer proposes that understanding a "text" involves a reciprocal relationship, similar to that of conversation partners, between the one trying to understand and the "text."[2] Thus, he uses the model of a genuine conversation to analyze the core process of understanding itself. The characteristics of a genuine conversation also apply to spiritual-direction conversations. These characteristics include (a) mutuality, (b) a question/answer structure, (c) a shared situation of "unknowing," (d) a non-adversarial climate, and (e) a specific subject matter of understanding.

The mutuality of the process is very important for Gadamer. Partners in a conversation do not intentionally confuse one another but try to ensure that they are following what each says. To do so, the speaker fills in necessary information and connections so the listener can "follow" the relationship of one idea to another or similarly follow the plot of a story. The listener tries to grasp the meaning communicated by the speaker, and initially asks questions to help clarify and verify the meaning. Rather than either of the participants directing the conversation, the subject matter does. The subject they pursue leads both partners.

Conversation is mutual because both persons are focused on the common subject and both help each other understand what is said. A shared situation of "unknowing" is also mutual. Even the person supposedly initiating the conversation does not know what might emerge from the conversation. Both partners contribute to the process, and neither knows what will "come out" by the end. Both partners share this indeterminacy about what might happen when they enter the conversation.

This mutual openness to what emerges within the conversation, however, is not necessarily a total indeterminacy. When one partner in a dialogue has greater knowledge of a particular subject than the other, the less knowledgeable person easily learns from or accedes to the other. In the case of spiritual direction, the directee may well recognize a director's more knowledgeable or experienced "judgment and insight and that for this reason his [or her] judgment takes precedence."[3] The directee as a partner in the conversation does not attribute authority to the director on the basis of role, but rather on the basis of the director's actual knowledge or experience as it is recognized in the conversation. Sam, the first story of spiritual direction presented in the previous chapter, describes learning from his director this way. It's repeated here:

> There was a serious question as to where our community would be living the next year, and direction helped me to separate my personal authority issues from those involving community politics. My director's experience as a woman religious who has been through her own battles was very helpful here.

> Through talking about the personal and political
> aspects of decision making about community hous-
> ing, I got to the point where I could lay this issue
> aside and not take the whole thing personally.

In this example, Sam gave authority to his director on the
basis of her lived experience. In the course of the conversation, however, his understanding of himself shifted so that
he claimed his own authority in a fresh way.

In addition, genuine conversation requires a friendly,
non-adversarial climate. The partners are not "out-arguing"
each other but weighing one another's opinion—testing out
what is being said. This testing occurs through questioning.
The questions reveal the truth or the strength of the other
rather than the weakness. This form of questioning seeks the
common ground of truthful agreement that forms the basis
of an emerging common meaning.

This search for the positive contribution of each partner
correlates to the question and answer dialectic that Gadamer
describes as an essential part of genuine conversation. Such
questioning asks: "Could this be the case?...If so, how?...
Might there be something else going on?" What emerges from
this kind of dialogue is something new that belongs to neither partner alone—shared meaning. Arriving at a common
understanding requires commitment to the truth that is
emerging about the subject they are pursuing together. They
cannot achieve this if they are only concerned about expressing themselves or imposing their own viewpoints.[4]

Spiritual Direction as Interpretive Conversation

Spiritual-direction conversations are fruitful when the
above conditions for conducting a "real" conversation occur.
However, the subject (topic) is the religious experience of the
person seeking direction and its implications for the life and

action of the directee. Thus, the person seeking direction focuses the conversation on his or her experience. This conversation is mutual in the sense that both director and directee are trying to understand the latter's descriptions or explanations of experience. The directee confirms or challenges the director's initial understandings. The conversation, however, is not entirely mutual because the director usually does not present his or her personal experiences for mutual understanding in this conversation. The focus is on the mutual understanding of the directee's experience and understandings.

The nature of religious experience itself, likewise, places both the director and the directee in a condition of indeterminacy. The director cannot know better than the directee what he or she has experienced. The director can invite the directee to understand and so more accurately interpret these experiences by exploring some events more fully than others. Fruitful spiritual-direction conversations, however, often leave both the director and the directee surprised by the outcome. In spiritual direction, both the person seeking direction and the director learn in the process.

An adversarial climate, as already noted, discourages this kind of collaborative process. Any significant self-disclosure about personal experiences or valued ideas requires receptivity. In spiritual direction, this quality is particularly necessary so that the directee feels sufficiently welcomed to share intimate or even challenging experiences of God. Frequently, such delicate experiences are only partially sensed by the directee who may feel unsure, challenged, or perplexed about them. Only a non-adversarial, collaborative climate welcomes the self-disclosure and exploration of not-yet-fully understood and appropriated experiences.

The question-and-answer structure of dialogue is also characteristic of the spiritual-direction conversation. Generally, the person seeking direction starts the conversation and initiates the topic(s) for a particular session. Frequently, the subject matter begins as a narrative of one or several experiences that have occurred since the last conversation. The director's questions may elicit either greater narrative detail—such as an expansion of what happened or another narrative describing something from the person's history that would illuminate this incident—or the directee's thoughts and feelings about the event. These questions help clarify the narrative or discover the implications for the directee through this shared exploration. Thus, the narratives created in spiritual direction emerge as answers to questions that arise within the conversation.

Role of Tradition

As seen in the introduction, the practice of spiritual direction has a long and varied history within Christian tradition, which recognizes it as an important spiritual practice. In fact, most major religious traditions have developed some form of one-to-one spiritual guidance. And in the contemporary period, spiritual direction is increasingly expanding into an interfaith context. Gadamer recognizes that tradition(s) within which human persons function condition human experience itself and shape attitudes and behavior. The historical models of spiritual direction illustrate this feature well. Contemporary spiritual direction is derived from earlier historical models, while contributing something entirely new to this tradition. According to Gadamer, a tradition is not only something received through historical transmission, but also something to which persons creatively contribute and expand. Thus, there is an element of creative freedom as well as historical continuity in tradition.[5]

Spiritual direction participates in two distinct yet related traditions. It is an ancient Christian practice originating from specialized forms of religious living. It is also deeply shaped by the narrative practices of Christianity embodied in its scriptures, rituals, and catechesis,[6] as well as by the Western literary tradition of spiritual and secular autobiography. The sacred tales that directees tell in spiritual-direction conversations take place within an already "storied" tradition. This storied tradition influences both the person seeking spiritual direction and the director through the shared narrative of Jesus' life, death, and resurrection; of his parables and teachings; and, in a sense, of Christian salvation history that reaches back into the narratives of the Hebrew Scriptures and strains forward through the age of the church to the end times.[7] Directors and directees from different Christian denominations are educated slightly differently in these stories because of historical differences in emphasis and in contemporary practice.

Christian tradition, which continues to express the shared faith of the community through its stories and through their enactment in ritual, considers the personal history of the individual as well as that of the community to be religiously significant. Christian tradition firmly believes that the God-human encounter takes place in and through human history. The entire biblical tradition expresses a shared experience and vision of the God-human relationship: God offers us a relationship with God's self that unfolds in time and respects human freedom and growth. Narrative is the linguistic form that best allows persons to share this kind of experience with one another.[8] Not surprisingly, the biblical authors were among the first to develop the skills of prose fiction because their theological perspective required it for telling their communal story.

Scripture scholar and literary critic Robert Alter, in his sensitive treatment of the art of narrative in the Hebrew Scriptures, makes this point. Only by developing the resources of prose fiction could the sacred writers depict their religious vision with both the precision and subtlety it demanded. Alter thinks that only a "fictionalized" history renders the nature of the God-human relationship most effectively.

> The implicit theology of the Hebrew Bible dictates a complex moral and psychological realism in biblical narrative because God's purposes are always entrammeled in history, dependent on the acts of individual men and women for their continuing

realization. To scrutinize biblical personages as fictional characters is to see them more sharply in the
multifaceted, contradictory aspects of their human
individuality, which is the biblical God's chosen
medium for his experiment with Israel and history.[9]

Although not every narrative technique used by Semitic
authors found its way into the Western tradition, critics have
long recognized that the literary form of prose fiction developed by biblical authors exerted a profound influence on the
development of fiction.[10] The Christian narrative tradition
and the Western secular literary tradition combined to provide the religious and cultural context for creating a certain
form of personal narrative or life story in spiritual direction.

The narrative form of spiritual autobiography, invented
by St. Augustine in his famous *Confessions*, has most directly
influenced the spiritual-direction narrative. Augustine adopts
from Roman prose the literary form of the journey, a narrative of dramatic outer events, and applies it to the drama and
intensity of his inner life.[11] Augustine shifts the drama of salvation history to its microcosmic form, showing how it plays
out in his personal life. This personal focus expresses the
Christian conviction that every person has unique worth and
value because God is concerned with each of us. Spiritual
direction encourages the person seeking direction to create a
unique oral narrative of his or her salvation history.

As we have seen, the role that tradition plays within the
spiritual-direction conversation is complex and multifaceted.
The "traditions" that influence the director and the person
seeking direction are constantly, although not always consciously, influencing the process of understanding and interpreting experience. Tradition, according to Gadamer, creates
further complexity through the "prejudices" it elicits and the
"horizon of meanings" involved in the process of understanding. Gadamer asserts that a person who seeks to understand something necessarily brings "pre-understandings"
—preconceptions—to current experience. A person always
projects some meaning or coherence onto the subject as soon

as an initial meaning emerges. This initial guessing at this initial meaning happens precisely because we already have some kind of expectation. However, this is a fluid process because we must constantly revise these initial preconceptions or expectations based on what actually emerges. The one trying to understand frequently is surprised and must then anticipate or project a different meaning.

Gadamer does not view prejudices, or pre-understandings, as essentially negative, but as a necessary part of the process for understanding to occur at all. However, we must replace these prejudices with more suitable ones in order to remain open to the meaning of the other person or the text. These preconceptions exist as anticipatory ideas, theories, story lines; we need to become aware of them consciously when the novelty of what we are trying to understand challenges us. The subject matter of understanding must be able to assert its truth against these pre-understandings and change them.[12] Likewise, as a director listens to a directee's narrative, he or she must continually revise these anticipated meanings and plot development in the light of the directee's actual story.

In the spiritual-direction conversation, the director and the person seeking direction usually share a complex set of prejudices, or pre-understandings, which not only come from a common culture and a shared historical moment but also come from the larger Christian tradition. This tradition will have shaped the spiritual life, practices, and theology of both persons. Because many of these assumptions are rooted in a common source, one can say that the tradition itself provides a context of shared prejudices. Insofar as both people tacitly agree with these shared preconceptions, neither of them may become conscious of them during the conversation. These pre-understandings usually become explicit when they prove inadequate in interpreting new experiences.

These shared prejudices from Christian tradition simply demonstrate the historical, social, and cultural nature of human consciousness. These shared prejudices contribute to forming a horizon of common meaning for the conversation.

Gadamer discusses "horizon of meaning" precisely in terms of historical consciousness. The times in which one lives limits what contemporaries can see from this perspective. A horizon is "the range of vision that includes all that can be seen from a particular vantage point."[13] Consequently, the horizon of a text from an earlier period of history is limited to its own horizon. In attempting to understand a text or a piece of art produced in another temporal horizon, we constantly move back and forth from the present to what we know about the past. The interpreter tries to appreciate the earlier horizon (what the *writer* could see) and yet may also experience a fusion of an earlier horizon with his or her own, so that a fresh meaning for the present can emerge. In this fusion, the interpreter can never completely leave his or her own horizon behind. Rather, one's own horizon expands to include the horizon of the other.

> English professor Barrett J. Mandel provides an example of how a reader finds present meaning in an autobiography written by someone in a different temporal horizon. Often the reader simply cannot know whether what he [or she] is reacting to is actually implied by the text or whether the text has triggered associations in the reader's own horizon. But it is this very overlapping of the autobiographer's and the reader's horizons that adds to the undeniable aura of truthfulness surrounding the text. In fact, it may be said that the reader projects truthfulness from his or her own body of assumptions or that he or she allows the text to manifest itself at the level of the truth.
>
> ...For me these profound moments body forth a sense of my sharing life—being—with the author, no matter how remote he or she may be from me in some ways. The autobiographer springs open a door and gives me a glance into his or her deepest reality, at the same time casting my mind into a state of reverie or speculation....It is the moment

Teresa of Avila experiences when she reads the garden scene in St. Augustine's *Confessions*: "When I began to read the *Confessions*, I thought I saw myself there described, and began to recommend myself greatly to this glorious Saint. When I came to his conversion, and read how he heard that voice in the garden, it seemed to me nothing less than that our Lord had uttered it for me: I felt so in my heart, I remained for sometime lost in tears, in great inward affliction and distress." At such a moment, St. Teresa's language merges with that of St. Augustine who seems to be speaking not only to her but in her, merging the particulars of his past with the particulars of hers and creating a moment of transcendence.[14]

This quotation also shows how readers might experience a text, deeply responding to their own situation. Teresa identifies with Augustine's conversion story. It becomes a model for her conversion and actually initiates it. Within her horizon of meaning—which includes God's personal relationship with the reader as well as with the writer of the text—Teresa is touched not only by Augustine's sense of himself, but she also felt in her heart that God was addressing her through his words in this text. This is an example of a relatively common experience that might be brought to a spiritual-direction conversation: an experience of God addressing a directee through the spiritual practice of reading sacred scripture or some other spiritual text.

Both participants in the spiritual-direction conversation likely share a common temporal horizon. However, each may hold a narrower or broader horizon of their shared Christian tradition and perhaps quite different cultural horizons. Consequently, they need to understand these differences in order to foster mutual understanding. In addition to distinguishing differences between personal horizons, both director and directee may also fuse their horizons, just as Teresa did with Augustine. The director may discover God is relating to him or her through the sacred tale the directee tells.

Because the horizon of the past, which exists in the form of tradition, influences every human life, every contemporary horizon of meaning includes a historical dimension. Becoming aware of history in one's own consciousness means acquiring an ability to situate one's present moment in relationship to the tradition or the history out of which it emerges.[15] In the spiritual-direction conversation, one partner in the dialogue may have a greater facility for situating a given issue within an appropriate historical context of the spiritual tradition(s). One would hope that a spiritual director has sufficient knowledge of the history of spirituality, and of the variety of experiences and recorded wisdom within it, to help the person seeking direction develop a more adequate horizon for exploring a concrete situation in his or her life.

Long-standing traditions are complex and multifaceted. They are not only passed on from one generation to the next, but each generation and its cultural context contribute to the tradition as well as receive from it. A neglected or suppressed dimension of a tradition may be rediscovered or may appeal freshly to the present. Those who live within a tradition have an active relationship to it. A tradition not only shapes an individual's attitudes and behaviors; individuals in turn address questions to the tradition: "Tradition is not simply a precondition into which we come, we produce it ourselves, inasmuch as we understand, participate in the evolution of tradition and hence further determine it ourselves."[16] Thus people, reflecting on their experiences in spiritual direction, pose questions to the tradition. They are not simply determined by the seemingly monolithic claims of the existing received tradition.

The example of Beguine women might help illustrate this interactive relationship with the tradition of women's religious life. In the twelfth century, a religiously inspired women's movement arose in the Dutch-, Flemish-, and German-speaking countries of Europe. These women created a new form of religious life in which celibate women lived together in a district of a city, usually around a church. They were self-supporting through lace making or other work in textiles. They often cared for the sick, sometimes taught children, and lived singly in medieval apartments that they owned and that they passed on to one another through their wills when they died. They gathered together on Sundays for worship in the local church and for reflection on the scriptures. They tended to live an intense contemplative life as well as serve the larger community. Gradually, some of these Beguine groups lived together in buildings that shared common open space and that became distinct sectors of the city. This more independent style of religious life that was both contemplative and ministerial was eventually suppressed by church authorities, and the women were forced to join existing religious orders or create for themselves a more regulated communal form of religious life if they wished to continue to live a life consecrated to God.

Some groups of women religious today seem to have almost unconsciously reinvented this form of living as members of apostolic religious communities in response to their own need to balance contemplative prayer with ministerial service. Frequently, their ministries themselves require more flexible ways of living than fully communitarian religious life. In this instance, contemporary women religious discover their own continuity with an earlier life-form in the tradition, and so far are living ministerial religious life in ways quite similar to the Beguines. Unlike the Beguines, they remain vowed members in religious institutes. Likewise, within the tradition of spiritual direction, Beguine women exercised a non-monastic model of spiritual direction and spiritual formation within these flexibly organized groups of women. Today, many religious women offer spiritual direction to a wide variety of people drawing on their contemplative experience, spiritual formation, and theological training.

This reciprocal relationship between the tradition and persons who stand within it is especially important in a historical period like our own in which reflection on certain contemporary experiences inspires some to either renew or reform a tradition. The Christian tradition, for example, has not adequately welcomed or even preserved the contribution of women because of the patriarchal and androcentric bias governing the "traditioning" process itself, within Roman Catholicism in particular.[17] Women's contributions to the Christian mystical tradition are better represented than their contributions in other traditions within Christianity, but even in this case their contributions usually entered the tradition only through male sponsorship and/or censorship and consequently may not encompass the full range of experience of even these remarkable women.

Contemporary spiritual direction may be a means of contributing to the Christian tradition as it welcomes into conversation narratives of the actual religious experience of women and men...lay, religious, and clerical...married and single from diverse cultures. If, as Gadamer claims, one's relationship with the tradition is truly reciprocal—if one is not only addressed by the tradition but also shapes it—then new strands of the spiritual tradition may well enrich Christian tradition through the contemporary practice of spiritual direction.

Application

Finally, Gadamer emphasizes that understanding one's tradition means the ability to understand it and apply it in different situations: "Understanding is, then, a particular case of the application of something universal to a particular situation."[18] In exploring how application demonstrates understanding, Gadamer draws on Aristotle's analysis of *phronesis*, or practical knowledge, to show how a person functions in a practical, moral way.[19] The practice of spiritual direction requires a similar ability to recognize the appropriate action required by a particular situation.

Aristotle distinguishes between theoretical knowledge and practical knowledge. One acquires practical knowledge in and through action, through participation and engagement, through the process of character development over one's lifetime. Practical knowledge consists of more than a "skill," which one can acquire and then forget. *Phronesis* is not something that can be forgotten, because it becomes part of one's accumulated life experience.

In order to discern a correct or appropriate course of action in the varied circumstances of life, one must develop and accurately apply practical knowledge to each situation. But *phronesis* is not something one has: it must be determined within the situation in which one must act. One learns how to act in the light of what is morally right. This kind of "seeing" and interpretation embraces both the means and the end. Its opposite consists of an inability to recognize that a situation calls for action of a moral nature. This practical kind of knowledge exemplifies for Gadamer how application is integral to understanding itself. If one cannot make an appropriate application, one really does not understand. In the case of practical knowledge, one doesn't first master principles and then apply them. Rather application codetermines understanding as a whole from the beginning.

The understanding (both the director's and the directee's) in the spiritual-direction conversation is eminently practical. Among other things, directees want to understand what their unique circumstances require of them. In the case of spiritual direction, the requirements are not restricted simply to the morally good thing to do, as in Aristotle's discussion of ethics and *phronesis*. In spiritual direction, directees not only confront choices about the moral good, but also about choices among several morally good things to do or ways to respond in particular situations. Directees seek to understand and respond to their experience of God calling and inviting them through their graced religious histories and life circumstances to appropriate choices and actions. Thus, growth in discernment among morally good actions is fostered in spiritual direction. This implies growth in the practical ability to correctly apply the "rules for discernment of spirits" of St. Ignatius or other classic guides for discernment.

Sam, from the previous chapter, exercised this kind of

practical knowledge when deciding whether or not to apply for ordination to the priesthood. To make this decision, he first had to reflect on his experience of formation and the novitiate, on his consistent relationship to God throughout this time, and on his desire to respond to this concretely experienced invitation. His experience at the diaconal ordination ceremony exemplifies the pattern of call and response as he understood it. Second, he had to rule out reasons motivated by fear or by some other lack of freedom. This he did by contrasting ordination as a priest with life as a partnered gay man. In this way, he could discover if his choice for celibate ordination in community was motivated primarily by fear of other life options. Sam also needed to rule out any hesitations based on psychological constraints. His strong desire or need to "be ready" reflected his need to be in control of his life beyond what was necessary at this time. He confronted this dynamic by exploring some of its contributing causes and realizing that they lacked persuasiveness. Finally, he needed to reflect on what was happening in psychoanalysis and decide whether it raised any issues that would suggest he should delay the decision or reexamine his vocational motivation.

The narrative detail Sam gave about his experience made it possible for the director to grasp the particular circumstances of his situation and the choices implicitly facing him. Understanding his unique situation, she could nurture his own practical knowledge in the context of his experience. In the second story of spiritual direction from the previous chapter, Mary wondered if she should become a religious after the failure of her marriage. Drawing on his practical knowledge of her and others, her director knew that this possibility was probably incongruous and perhaps a fantasy of escape from her pain. From this key event in her retreat, Mary learned something about the principle of Ignatian discernment that cautions against making decisions in a state of desolation.

This practical kind of participation in another's life grows out of the bond established between the director and the directee. It assumes that the director wants what the directee wants most deeply: to do what God wants. The director thus "thinks with the other and undergoes the situation with him or her."[20] This capacity to experience another's situation frequently results from imaginative participation in the other's narrative—a version of accurate empathy.[21]

Directees often seek such practical assistance through spiritual direction. The director is committed to supporting and promoting the directee's spiritual growth and discerning choices. The director is allied with helping the directee become the person he or she desires to be. For each directee, this is an intensely personal experience. Both the director and the directee tend to grow in concrete and practical ways. The director helps each directee respond to his or her particular situations, helps each discern among possible good choices, and helps each grow in the ability to act on that knowledge. As the director works with different people and responds to their particular situations, he or she gradually develops his or her own practical knowledge as a spiritual director.

Gadamer's characterization of *phronesis* as the interplay, not only between principles and their application, but also between the goal of becoming a good person and actually realizing it is relevant to spiritual direction. The dialectical interplay between knowledge and application is an ongoing, self-revising process. A person bases his or her understanding of what a "good" person would do on the experience of other people, as well as on his or her ideal of the virtuous person. But only by actually making virtuous choices does someone truly understand why that action is virtuous and how it affects the moral agent. The spiritual director does not make moral choices for the directee; rather the director's role is to foster the directee's growth in moral agency. Thus, the director helps the directee reflect on possible courses of action, and when the directee arrives at a decision, this reflection continues from the new perspective of action.

David Tracy and Johann Baptist Metz

The theological hermeneutics of David Tracy emphasizes the analogical imagination. Political theologian Johann Baptist Metz emphasizes the principle of listening to the narrative voices of those who suffer and of hearing them as a *memoria passionis* ("memory of Christ's passion") that is present in human history long after Jesus. These two theologians make questions of interpretation more concrete and poignant in the present moment; that is, how do we experience the religious dimension of life?

Tracy pays close attention to basic human experience and religious language in order to understand the religious dimension in Christian experience. He first turned to the phenomenology of "limit-experiences" and then complemented them with experiences of "self-transcendence," or ecstatic experiences that invite a basic trust in the face of mystery. Tracy tends to maintain a constant dialectic between the negative and the positive poles of experience. Karl Jaspers was the first to name "limit-experiences"—such as sickness, guilt, anxiety, and the recognition of death—as "boundary situations." These existential experiences confront us with our deep vulnerabilities and mortality. Tracy says they "disclose to us either a faith or an unfaith in the meaningfulness of life."[22] This is the negative pole to our experience that may push us deeper into God or into unbelief. They are complemented by the positive pole of ecstatic experiences such as joy, authentic love, creativity, and so on, which are also "'common human experiences' and 'signals of transcendence' which invite a response of 'fundamental trust' in the face of mystery."[23]

In his hermeneutical reading of the New Testament, Tracy concluded that its diverse literary forms—"parables, narratives, proverbs, eschatological sayings—correlate with the limit-language and limit-experiences of common human experience. Religious language is imaginative, analogical, mystical, metaphorical, mythical, symbolic, and poetic."[24] Consequently, it "disorients us," "redescribes our experience," and "discloses a limit-referent which projects and promises that one can, in fact, live a life of wholeness, total commitment or radical honesty and agapic love in the presence of the gracious God of Jesus Christ."[25]

It follows then, that the spiritual-direction conversation invites the directee first to "story" such experience and then to explore it in the light of the story of Jesus: his life, ministry, teachings, stories, death, and resurrection, and the loving Mystery whom he invites us to trust. Metz, a student of Karl Rahner, poignantly describes how Rahner showed the connection between theology and "the mystical biography of the ordinary average Christian person...a Christian life without great transformations and conversions."[26] Rahner, according to Metz, tried to make this connection in his own faith experience, and then to foster in others the significance of "religious experience, the articulation of one's life story before God."[27]

The contemporary model of spiritual direction focuses on the religious experience of each directee, helping the person seeking direction to articulate his or her life story before God.

How Postmodern Are We?

David Tracy also tried to articulate the return of God in postmodern history, noting that everyone does not participate in nor embrace the mind-set commonly called postmodern with equal enthusiasm.

In the important essay "On Naming the Present," Tracy suggests that we really do not know how to name our present moment in history. The "we" faced with this challenge is, for him, the very Western "we" of Europe and North America. This "we" does not include all those peoples of the world whom "we" might recognize as the "other." In this situation, he says that some of us quite securely or insecurely inhabit modern consciousness—inhabit the sense of ourselves as independent, individual agents, shaping our own history and persisting in believing in a myth of progress, scientific development, and the pluralistic and democratic achievements rooted in Enlightenment thought. However, there still remain many persons and communities who might be classified as "antimoderns" who await the return of the traditional and communal self. These retreat to a nonexistent past and a nonhistorical "pure" tradition in the face of modernity and postmodernity. The postmoderns among us see through the myth of progress that has certainly neither delivered on its emancipatory promises nor achieved recognizable progress throughout the incredibly violent twentieth century; postmoderns place the "hope of the present in otherness and difference."[28] Tracy claims these others are those "marginalized groups of modernity and tradition alike—the mystics, the dissenters, the avant-garde artists, the mad, the hysterical."[29]

Tracy applauds the "new perspective" of those of us who inhabit the center of privilege and power in the West; however, he also recognizes that hidden within us remains the "secret wish that we [were] still the center and [could] name those others. The others remain at the margins."[30]

The "other" envisaged from that self-named center is too often a "projected" other. We project onto the "other" new fears of the loss of privilege and power of the modern bourgeois subject, or the hopes for another chance of the neoconservative, or the desires for escape from modernity of the postmodern non-self. A fact seldom admitted by the moderns, the antimoderns, and the postmoderns alike—even with all the talk of otherness and difference—is that there is no longer *a* center with margins. There are many centers. Our common task is to learn from all these centers characterized by difference rather than impose our projections upon them.

Tracy says that, as a consequence of this situation, we live in a time of "conflict of interpretations" about how to name the Western present and that each of these stances—modern, antimodern, and postmodern—refuses to "face the *fascinans et tremendum* actuality of our polycentric present."[31] At the same time, he says, despite fears of anarchy, we can each of us only "face this polycentrism from where we are." He then draws on the insights of political theologian Metz to assert that a path through this dilemma can be found in a "mystical-prophetic option" rooted within Christianity itself. Tracy says:

> To seize the heart of the matter of the Christian gospel in our present moment is to expose the false visions of the present which afflict us....We find, rather, the emergence of a mystical-prophetic option emerging in myriad theological forms in all the centers of our polycentric church, in the churches of Latin America, Asia, and Africa; in the movements for social and individual emancipation in the centers of Eastern and Central Europe; in the feminist theologies throughout the world; in the African American and Native American theologies of North America; in the rethinking of the indigenous traditions of South and Central America. We always live in a time of danger—as the repressed histories of the oppressed in every culture show, as the memory of the cross and resurrection of Jesus Christ insistently brings to the attention of every Christian generation.[32]

Tracy insistently turns our attention to a new sense of self that needs to emerge in the West on the basis of genuine engagement and dialogue with the prophetic voices that represent this history of suffering.

> The prophetic voices of our present may be found best, as they were for the ancient prophets and for Jesus of Nazareth, in those peoples, those individuals, and those new centers most privileged to God and still least heard in the contemporary Western conflict of interpretations of naming the present: the suffering and the oppressed.[33]

Despite the variety and conflict among these speakers, nevertheless, their emergence in the present makes them bold enough to "drink from their own wells," in the metaphor of Gustavo Gutiérrez. Tracy says that our response

> cannot be one of mere modern liberal guilt, but of Christian responsibility—capable of responding, critically when necessary, to the other as other and not as a projection of ourselves. The result could be a new solidarity in the struggle for the true time of justice and a communal, theological naming of the present in a polycentric world and a global church led by these new voices....[S]uch hope, grounded in the Pentecost of the time of the Spirit alive in many centers, does promise liberation for all. To resist ourselves and our present may be the first sign of that hope. To trust God—the living, judging, promising God of the prophets, mystics, and Jesus the Christ—to act on that trust is the surest sign of that hope. The mystics and prophets are alive in unexpected ways among us. A mystical-prophetic theology with many centers is being born around the globe....The true present is the present of all historical subjects in all the centers in conversation and solidarity before the living God.[34]

Finally, Tracy observes the strange return of God into postmodernity as interruption:

> —the interruption of massive global suffering in modern history and the interruption of all those others set aside, forgotten, and colonized by the grand narrative of Eurocentric modernity. The meaning of suffering, the reality of the others and the different: those are the realities that...allow for the return of the eschatological God disrupting all continuity and confidence....God enters postmodern history not as a consoling "ism" but as an awe-

some, often terrifying, hope-beyond-hope. God enters history again not as a new speculation...but as God. Let God be God becomes an authentic cry again. This God reveals God-self in hiddenness: in cross and negativity, above all in the suffering of all those others whom the grand narrative of modernity has set aside as non-peoples, non-events, non-memories, non-history.

God comes first as empowering hope to such peoples...a God promising to help liberate and transform all reality....[35]

God also comes to postmoderns as interruption,

as the hidden-revealed God of the hope of the cross, in the memory of suffering and the struggle by, for, and with "others"—especially the forgotten and marginal ones of history. God also comes as an ever deeper Hiddenness—awesome power, the terror, the hope beyond hopelessness often experienced in the struggle for liberation itself. Thus does the God of Job speak out of the whirlwind again....Thus does suffering unto God and lamentation toward God emerge as a resistance to all modern speculation on God in the post-Auschwitz, later political *theo-logia* of Johann Baptist Metz.[36]

In addition to the return of God through the interruption of human suffering in "the apocalyptic God of power, hope, and awe," the God of love "enters postmodernity first as transgression, then as excess, and finally as the transgressive excess of sheer gift." Tracy goes on to say that just as Job and Lamentations return in situations of interruption and suffering, "so too such texts as the Song of Songs and the feminist retrievals of God as Sophia return to be heard in ways modern theologies did not envisage as even possible, much less desirable. Desire, body, love, gift have all returned to allow God-as-God to be named anew."[37]

With these hermeneutical perspectives culled from Gadamer, Tracy, and Metz, we turn now to the narrative practice of spiritual direction in this very new context of plurality. It is important to recognize how we are shaped by our historical past, and it is important to recognize who arrives for spiritual direction—an antimodern, a modern, a postmodern, or one of the "others" from Western perspective—and the narrative form that his or her story takes.

Questions for Reflection

1. How does your directee encounter the living God in religious experiences encompassing both limit and ecstasy?

2. How is this self and God co-creating a new story in our times?

3. Is the practice of spiritual direction strengthening and confirming the historical subjectivity and liberating action of a formerly non-person?

Chapter Three
The Narrative Impulse in Human Experience

Chapter 2 described several important ideas from hermeneutics that help us see spiritual direction as a process of interpretation and self-understanding. Because directees tell their sacred tales in spiritual direction, this chapter reflects on the narrative impulse and its relationship to human experience.

In the last thirty years there has been an increasing appreciation for the role of narrative in human experience and in cross-disciplinary applications of narrative understandings of experience. These range from the retrieval of narrative in theology in order to correct an overemphasis on doctrinal formulations; to narrative psychology replacing a systems-theory approach in family therapy;[1] to the development of narrative methods of research in education, anthropology, psychology, and sociology.[2] In addition, biography and autobiography have become an intense focus for literary studies, as well as having spawned a new field called narrative studies.[3] Cognitive psychologist Jerome Bruner is among a growing number of theorists who now propose that telling and understanding a story is one form of thought that is complemented by another form—that of formulating arguments.[4] As Clandinin and Connolly discovered: "For us, life—as we come to it and as it comes to others—is filled with narrative fragments, enacted in storied moments of time and space, and reflected upon and understood in terms of narrative unities and discontinuities."[5]

Creating an internal narrative is the way we maintain a sense of continuity of ourselves through time; also, narrative is the only way we can share our experience with others.

Understanding the nature and importance of narrative is our first step toward appreciating why a narrative approach to spiritual direction is both desirable and beneficial.

Defining Narrative

Narrative as we are using it here refers to the storytelling that characterizes spiritual direction. We can describe the interaction between the director and the person seeking direction as a face-to-face narrative situation within the context of conversation in which the directee tells the sacred tales of his or her faith-filled life experiences. The director listens to this story and also influences its telling. As the usually solo audience, the director affects the story of the directee's experience both by the way she or he enters into the conversation (questions, interpretations, empathy) and by nonverbal responses (attention, facial expression, feelings).[6] The person seeking direction tells a religiously shaped life story, incorporating key episodes from the past and the present related to his or her understanding of spiritual direction. This graced story unfolds serially over time. These aspects of the storytelling situation give the resulting narrative distinctive features.[7]

Minimally, a narrative is a symbolic representation of events, connected (in the judgment of the speaker) by subject matter, related by time, and told to either an actual or an implied audience.[8] Most people, however, have more complex expectations of narrative:

- Some form of temporal sequencing
- Connections of events causally as well as chronologically or some other recognizable pattern
- Some reference to character and the world of human values
- Meaning or significance

To account for and to describe distinguishable elements of narrative, traditional literary criticism has developed the terms *plot, character, theme, narrative strategies, point of view, tone, author's voice, irony*, and *imagery*.[9]

In addition to sequence and pattern, narratives include both explanation and description.[10] Descriptive narratives invite the reader or listener into the setting (the social world and physical environment) of the narrator. For example, the reader/audience imagines what a character or a given setting looks like. Description draws the reader or listener cooperatively into the tale. Description reveals our attitudes, feelings, characteristic behaviors, and habits of responding to life experiences. Thus, descriptions disclose the narrator's "point of view"[11] and enable the storyteller to share with another the unique way he or she experiences life. Point of view, together with reports about action and behavior, reveals a great deal about a person's character. Spiritual direction is largely concerned with how the person seeking direction responds to religious experience and how that experience affects the directee's attitudes and responses to life. The directee's point of view that colors his or her descriptions allows the director to notice changes and continuity in the directee's perceptions and behavior.

Likewise, narrative includes elements of explanation that are embodied in the plot as well as in formal argument. Plot is itself a form of explanation; the plot in both its sequence and pattern explains why things turn out the way they do.[12] Explanations typically accompany this "explanation by emplotment."[13] Spiritual-direction conversations frequently involve two different types of explanation. Directees embody their explanations in the plots of their narratives, as well as through direct explanation. Psychologist James Hillman was among the first to propose that in psychoanalytic case histories—which he describes as fictions—"plots are our theories. They are the ways in which we put the intentions of human nature together so that we can understand the why between the sequence of events in story."[14]

This correlation between theory and emplotment suggests that other theories, not just the psychoanalytic one, may be woven into the spiritual-direction narrative through the combination of plot and narrator-offered explanation. For instance, a directee will incorporate his or her operative theology, such as a view of divine Providence, into the plot. He or she will tell how God's activity influences the events and relationships of life as part of the plot.

The interpretive theories of the director, likewise, influence his or her response to the directee's stories. If the director's guiding theory is theological, she or he will often identify for the directee the theological dimension related to the story just heard. The director might make a comment such as, "Your story seems to be about experiences of God's providential care surrounding your life." If influenced by a Jungian psychological theory, the listener might identify it as an experience of "synchronicity." Either interpretive response will then shape future stories.

Regardless of how different theorists describe the relationship between narrative activity and life experience, there is a relationship between fictional worlds and the world of human experience. Narrative conventions both mirror life patterns and bring greater coherency to less easily perceived patterns of life. We often assert in one way or another that people are themselves "stories." Our beginning is marked by birth, and the end by death, and the events in between are connected by both temporal sequencing and cause-and-effect relationships. People find themselves "in situations that they change or to whose changes they react. These changes in turn reveal hidden aspects of the situation and the characters of the people and give rise to a new predicament calling for thought or action or both. The response to this predicament brings the story to its conclusion."[15]

To compare human life itself to a story assumes that life has or can have a sense of continuity over a lifetime. Theologian Michael Novak suggests that "story" helps us achieve continuity: "A story is a structure for time. A story links actions over time. The more integrated a life, the more all things in it work toward a single (perhaps comprehensive) direction. The richer the life, the more subplots the story encompasses."[16] We, then, enact a story by our actions. When linked

71

together in an internal narrative, these create the continuity of personal identity, which itself is a narrative construction. In the next chapter, we will look more closely at the narrative construction of identity.

The Narrative Quality of Experience

In an important essay, philosopher Stephen Crites stated that "the formal quality of experience through time is inherently narrative."[17] He concluded that consciousness itself must have a narrative form corresponding to narrative forms of speech common to all cultures.[18] Indeed, consciousness is narrative. We are socialized in childhood into how to tell our personal stories and learn to create them by using the stories we are told, the stories we read, and the stories we observe in our culture.[19]

Transformative experiences, which alter our vision of reality, require a narrative that can integrate past and future with these new experiences. For this reason, spiritual direction encourages individuals to glimpse the coherence and significance of their religious experience and its impact on their personal histories partially through storying it.

Crites compared the narrative quality of experience to music. Organizing our lives through stories resembles the experience of music. Each event, each note, occurs in temporal succession, and we experience them as a unity only through time. The resulting form is "revealed only in the action as a whole."[20] In language, narrative is the form that is "capable of expressing coherence through time."[21]

Terrence Tilley, commenting on Crites's view, agrees that there are intrinsic links between narratives and experience:

If our experience is inherently durational, then we must use narrative to speak of it. Stories tell of a body individual or communal—embedded in a world.

72

They portray experience through time. Of course, stories without analysis and criticism are as dangerous as analysis without stories. When we lose our critical abilities our stories may be deformed, false, or damaging without our awareness of them.[22]

Crites thinks that we organize our experience in narrative, not only because temporal consciousness requires it, but also because a storied sense of reality continually shapes this consciousness. Somehow we live in a storied world too deep to tell. Crites names a consciousness-shaping story a *sacred story*. Such a story can never completely be put into words and is often enacted in ritual and dance and in other embodied ways within a community. Frequently, a sacred story is a creation story that actually creates the consciousness of those who live within this particular story. Crites also uses the term *mundane story* for those stories we consciously use and tell. With the increase in globalization and our exposure to the world-creating stories of others, we begin, perhaps, to sense our own more clearly.[23] Crites concludes that consciousness itself must have a narrative form if it serves to mediate between the narrative shaping of consciousness and our personal and collective elaboration of narratives.[24] We experience temporality through an always-interrelated sense of past, present, and future. Only the present moment actually exists, and we exist in it in relationship to the past and an anticipated future.[25]

Before we can understand the complex relationship of past, present, and future, we need to look at the role of memory. In its simplest form, autobiographical memory gives coherence to the moment-by-moment perceptions, feelings, and thoughts that constitute conscious experience by simply providing what appears to be an image stream in temporal succession. Often we do little more than reconstruct a simple memory from this flux of experience. Without this rudimentary temporal memory, all experience would be locked into a fragmentary present unconnected to past or future. However, memory is more complex than simple recall, for it also enables us to reorder past experiences and recollect the images in constantly new patterns. To tell a story drawing from one's "stored memory bits" requires more than a recital of the constantly reconstructed pieces of our reactivated autobiographical memories. Telling a significant story, selecting a key episode from our autobiographical memory, is one of the most common ways of recalling an experience and reconstructing our memories of an event.

The following example from Crites's work clarifies the differences between consulting the temporally sequenced information from the core self and incorporating it into autobiographical memory to create constantly new interpretations in the retelling of an experience. Crites, however, notes that there are limits to creating a new story on the basis of later experience and knowledge. There are details in our memory that need to be honored in every telling. Otherwise, we have begun to create a fictional story rather than an autobiographical one. Crites writes:

> I recall, for example, a sequence from my own memory.[26] In telling its course, recollection already intervenes, but I recollect in a way as faithful as possible to memory itself. I measure out "a long time" and recall an episode from my childhood. I have not thought about it for many years, and yet I find its chronicle in good condition, extremely detailed and in clear sequence. In an impetuous fit of bravado I threw a rock through a garage window. I recall the exact spot on the ground from which I picked up the rock. I recall the windup, the pitch, the rock in midair, the explosive sound of the impact, the shining spray of glass, the tinkling hail of shards falling on the cement below, the rough, stony texture of the cement. I recall also my inner glee at that moment, and my triumph when a playmate, uncertain at first how to react, looked to me for his cue and then broke into a grin. Now I could cut and splice a bit, passing over hours not so clearly

recalled anyway, except that my mood underwent drastic change. Then I recall that moment in the evening when I heard my father's returning foot-steps on the porch and my guilty terror reached a visceral maximum the very memory of which wrenches a fat adult belly—for remembering is not simply a process in the head. The details of the scene that ensued are likewise very vivid in my memory.

Now it would be quite possible for me to tell this story very differently. My perspective on it has been changed, partly by the death of my father and the fact that I am now myself the father of children, partly, too, by my reading in the *Confessions* a story about a wanton theft of pears and by some reading in Freud on the rivalry of fathers and sons, and so forth. So I have many insights into this chronicle that I could not have had at the time its events occurred. Yet the sophisticated new story I might tell about it would be superimposed on the image-stream of the original chronicle. It could not replace the original without obliterating the very materials to be recollected in the new story. Embedded in every sophisticated retelling of such a story is this primitive chronicle preserved in memory. Even con-scious fictions presuppose its successive form, even when they artfully reorder it.[27]

The narrative form of consciousness also includes the constantly experienced relationship between past, present, and future. These three modalities are present and related to one another in every moment of experience. The present exists only in relationship to the past out of which it emerges and also stands in relationship to the future that we can anticipate in the present. Like Crites, one can refer to the rudimentary narrative form for the future, which corre-sponds to the narrative form of memory for the past, as a "scenario of anticipation." By projecting courses of action, we imagine a variety of possible stories about the future. These scenarios of the future lack the density of detail of our stories of the past, and frequently the future turns out rather differently from our projected stories about it. Scenarios of anticipation, nevertheless, relate to the remembered past, especially through the sense of the self we project into the future. This sense of self that provides a sense of continuity of self from the past and present is a person's narratively constructed identity.

Despite the continuity between the past and the future, these temporal modes of experience remain clearly distinct from one another. The past is over, completed. Its events and actions cannot be undone on the level of factual deed. We can only change the story of our past by reinterpreting it or retelling it from the perspective of new experience in the present.[28]

Conversion stories provide classic religious examples of retelling and reinterpreting the past based on an experience or understanding unavailable to the person during the actual events of the past. Augustine in the *Confessions* clearly retells the whole of his life from his newly assimilated perspective of Christian faith. The significance of past events may change, but the events themselves do not. Just as the past is determinate, the future is as yet indeterminate.

Although the past continues to determine present experience,[29] the present is the decisive moment in an unfolding story. Indeed, it constitutes the moment of action in relationship to past and future. Thus, the narrative quality of experience can only occur in the present moment. Only in and from the present do we remember the past, experience the present, and anticipate the future. For the present is the temporal and physical location of embodied human experience.[30]

Our spiritual-direction stories reflect this embodiment. The communication between director and directee is always immediately embodied. The directee as narrator tells his or her story out loud, using body language as well as words to communicate experience. Facial expression, physical movement, voice, eye contact, physical sensations related to affect—

all contribute to the storytelling process. Crites's memory of breaking the garage window was so vividly associated with viscerally felt intense emotion that he still remembers his physical sensations.

How directees enter the room and sit down, for instance, reflects their attitude and how safe or trusting they feel in the director's presence. One directee took eight months to move from the far cushion on the couch to the one directly facing me. I interpreted this gradual change in physical position to indicate increasing trust and comfortableness with himself and with me in the direction process.

Finally, as Crites demonstrated in his story of breaking a garage window, we know and express feelings in a physical way. In spiritual direction, feelings become present in a fully embodied way as people talk about past experiences, although the current feelings are not necessarily identical to remembered ones. This process of communication and interaction is fully embodied for both persons. Directees are also moved to tears when they tell stories of suffering and of compassion for others, and they come alive bodily in amazing ways while sharing other themes in their stories. A directee frequently knows and consciously experiences physical and emotional reactions to narrated events before being able to identify them verbally. The director also experiences the directee's narrative performance physically. The director receives the directee's story through bodily perception and relies on a felt bodily sense of the person's narrative in and through his or her embodied form of knowing.

Life imitates art and art represents life. Our narrative form of consciousness proves far more rudimentary in pattern and sequence than any fully articulated narrative. The tightly organized plots and motifs of artful stories help us give greater coherence to the more inchoate pattern and sequence of our more diffuse consciousness.[31] People do not acquire their stories apart from social context and history. Michael Novak puts it this way: "How does one acquire a story? The culture in which one is born already has an image of time, of the self, of heroism, of ambition, of fulfillment. It burns its heroes and archetypes deeply into one's psyche."[32]

Narrative and Metaphorical Expression of Experience

Experience

Human experience is an interpretive encounter with someone or something and a reflective, conceptual awareness of this encounter. As Denis Edwards defines it: "Experience is best seen as encounter with some thing or person which has become available to consciousness through reflective awareness. It refers to an encounter that is interpreted within human consciousness. This second element, interpretation, has always already occurred whenever we know we have experienced something."[33] According to this understanding, the interpretive element does not occur in a moment of subsequent reflection, but the "interpreting self precedes the encounter, enters into the encounter, and reflects upon the encounter."[34] This approach to interpretation supports the comments above about how the story we create out of our experience already includes an interpretation and an understanding of the experience.

Assimilating the effects and grasping the implications of experiences that affect us deeply require further reflection and interpretation. This subsequent reflection depends on the "richly nuanced totality in which experience, thought and interpretation run together in the same way as past, present and expectations of the future."[35] One can always distinguish between the original experience and later reflection, but we frequently sense that the original experience is too rich, too full of multiple meanings, to be accounted for adequately in conceptual language alone.

Philosopher Michael Polanyi developed the concept of "tacit" knowing to describe nonconceptual forms of knowing that might apply to some experiences that are difficult to put into words. Such tacit knowing is based on the kind of knowing related to developing a skill. Phenomenologically, understanding many varieties of human experience involves sensory, conceptual, and skill factors. In any given experience one of these factors will predominate although the other factors may also be present. In terms of spiritual direction, the "tacit," preconceptual, or skill mode may be most helpful.[36] Polanyi's notion of "tacit" knowing recognizes the form of knowing entailed in performing a craft. We cannot learn or teach a skill through concepts alone; much of what we genuinely know in the practical performance of a task we cannot really express in words.[37]

Understanding experiences of love, beauty, music, and God draw on this skill mode of knowing. We cannot reduce these encounters to concepts or words. Although we use concepts, images, and words to speak about them, something in these encounters exceeds our linguistic ability. For example, the experience of a beautiful piece of music transcends the sounds themselves and the structure of the music. The apprehension of beauty in the music results from the individual elements as well as from the experience of the music as a whole. This "musical way of knowing" also builds up over time as we experience different performances and become experienced in music appreciation and listening. We apprehend beauty in a preconceptual form. Similarly, what we ordinarily call an experience of God is usually an awareness of God that is limited neither to sensory nor to intellectual factors, but is, nonetheless, present in awareness. If our experience of God over time is preconceptual or "tacit," there are always some aspects of it that cannot be put into words but that are, nonetheless, real.

Expressing Experience

Human experience[38] is a personal encounter with someone or something—a reality that may be external to the self but that becomes available to consciousness. Of itself, experience has a temporal quality to it; to become "experienced" is a process that takes place in a cumulative fashion over time. Most of us automatically tell a story to share an experience. When asked, "What happened or what was your experience?" most of us launch into a story. The narrator recounts the events usually in the temporal order in which things unfolded, usually accompanied by the narrator's thoughts about the event and the feelings evoked by it. Frequently we tell a story of an experience to share our wisdom or to secure a witness to our experience. We invite the listener to participate imaginatively in our experience and judge its plausibility. Effective narration is one way we persuade the listener of the truth of our assertions about the event in question.[39] For instance, Evelyn, a former student, perceptively describes her desire for affirmation and witness in spiritual direction:

> In spiritual direction my experience is witnessed and affirmed. Primarily, I mean my spiritual experiences; but since these are often part of everyday, ordinary life, or they are intertwined with ordinary life, spiritual direction affirms my life as sacred and helps me explore that further. In spiritual direction, I articulate my experiences and my relationship with God in a setting, with a person, who holds them sacred and honors them. This names them sacred in the community, not just privately, which helps me own them more fully.

We rely on narrative to communicate the most mundane kind of "news." Even in our highly visual culture, all news coverage must contain what happened to someone at a specific time and place and provide some reason why it happened. Pictures without narrative accompaniment are not enough to tell the story. Narrative, thus, reconstructs a plausible set of events in temporal sequence in order to explain, if not *why* something happened, at least *what* happened. All reportage, then, is narrative in this simple way. Narrative, by its nature, invites the imaginative participation of its audience. Listeners/viewers vicariously accumulate new experiences as well as give the narrator an opportunity to make those same experiences more concrete through telling. Within a religious context, narrative is the primary form for communicating a tradition, even when narratives of original experiences of faith embody that tradition anew or challenge it to change.

The spiritual-direction conversation encourages directees to share their unique experiences of faith. These sacred tales are often difficult to tell. As storyteller and pastor William Bausch says:

> Story, with all of its literary metaphors, symbols, images, and figures of speech, is the first and the best expression of the inexpressible. Story uses every art at its disposal to say the unsayable. In story, it's not what the words say—those wild images and metaphors—but what they symbolize....People tell stories because that's the closest they can come to indicating mystery and uncovering truth. Story is truth's natural home.[40]

By telling the story of how they have encountered the mysteries of faith, directees make their experiences increasingly specific, coherent, personal, and concrete. As a result, they often discover more intensely the religious dimension of reality permeating ordinary experience. The directee's consciousness of God's presence at times may be very subtle and elusive, while at others, almost impossible to ignore. The spiritual director can encourage the expression and appropriation of these religious experiences by selectively eliciting stories and descriptions that portray the interactions between God and the directee. The purpose of this elaboration of the story helps the directee carefully notice what is happening in the God-human relationship.[41] Once the directee can notice and express what is going on, the director can then explore possible implications for the directee.

Telling these sacred tales in spiritual direction encourages the directee to share the experience in chronological order, incorporating into this story his or her thoughts, feelings, actions, and reactions. Incoherence or confusion in the narrative indicates elements of the experience that the directee has not yet appropriated or sufficiently understood. Clues within the verbal composition and its oral delivery—voice tone, pauses, the search for words, rushes of words—guide the director in deciding what parts of the story or how it was told require comment, analysis, or elicitation of more detail.

In addition, the oral and spontaneous nature of these narratives tends to give them a diffuse character. Although the directee does select and shape the stories, material that he or she would most likely omit from a written composition or a rehearsed oral composition often escapes into the narrative and becomes available for development or comment by the director. Because the storyteller is involved in a face-to-face process, it is not uncommon for a directee spontaneously to tell a different story than initially planned or, in response to the director's questions, to tell a background story that helps the director understand how this new event fits into the directee's larger life story. One story illuminates another. Thus the directee's entire life story is the primary interpretive background for each new life chapter. It is not uncommon for a director to be unaware of major life events of the directee until a new experience brings up an earlier story that sheds light on the new one.

Some spiritual directors may be tempted to make the point that directees could just as well write a lyric poem in order to share religious experience rather than rely on narrative. Although some directees do bring a poem, a painting, or a musical composition related to a significant religious experience to spiritual direction, these artistic representations usually relate to a very specific mystical experience in the course of a retreat or of ordinary daily life and most do not rely on them as their primary mode of expression.[42] Poet Charles Simic explains, "Nowhere else in literature does one find the experience of living in the moment so vividly rendered as in lyric poetry."[43] The selective nature of these artistic forms seems less helpful than narrative in the initial exploration of an experience in spiritual direction. The tightly unified expression of the lyric form excludes all seemingly extraneous details. As a result of this conscious artistic selectivity, the director has less access to aspects of the experience the directee could not assimilate into this compressed artistic form.

Limitations of poetic or other artistic forms in the context of spiritual direction do not imply that they are unimportant for many directees. They simply capture and express different aspects of the experience. Nonnarrative artistic expressions often are quite useful *after* an initial exploration of the experience. These forms become a way of crystallizing the most significant aspect of the experience, which may have become clearer because of the attempts to narrate it first. Lyric or graphic expression becomes a way of appropriating the experience more deeply. The following example from a spiritual-direction conversation may clarify the difference.

On the third or fourth day of a directed retreat, Linda, a religious sister, started talking to the director about the gift of friendship with a priest, instead of describing her prayer experience from the previous day. As she talked, she appeared shy and slightly flushed. Initially, the director was puzzled: Why was this topic coming up at this point in the retreat? What had evoked the memory of this friendship and Linda's emotional and reflective preoccupation with it?

The director first invited a general description of the friendship. Linda described a pleasant, emotionally supportive relationship that involved going out to dinner a couple of times a year and exchanging letters three or four times. She had not seen Tom recently, nor did she frequently fantasize about him. The emotional intensity of Linda's relationship with Tom did not seem to account for her thinking about him most of the day.

When the director then asked Linda to describe what happened before she began to reminisce about her friend, she said that she had been sitting under a tree, quietly attentive to God. In the midst of her prayer, she began to experience feelings of love and mild sexual sensations. It seemed to be this gentle upsurge of erotic and romantic, loving feelings that had initiated the reverie and subsequent reflection about her friend.

Because Linda had never noticed erotic or romantic feelings in prayer, she attached them to her friendship with Tom. When the director wondered if her sexual feelings might have been a response to the loving and intimate quality of God's presence to her in the retreat, she visibly relaxed and felt that might be true. She appeared to be less perplexed about her experience and shifted her attention back to God with whom she was becoming more intimately involved.

If Linda had written a poem, it would have been about her friendship with Tom. Starting from that poem, the director might have found it difficult to uncover with Linda the experience that had evoked her romantic feelings. Instead, simply by narratively reconstructing the events, Linda discovered for herself that she had mistaken the source of her feelings. Her director then helped her find a more appropriate horizon of meaning in which to situate her experience by connecting her story to the mystical tradition, especially the writings of Teresa of Avila and John of the Cross. When Linda understood more accurately what had evoked her feelings, she responded immediately in her prayer the next day as well as incorporated both experiences of love into a new narrative.

This example clarifies the narrative component in the spiritual-direction conversation. In Linda's case, about half of this session was spent eliciting a narrative that explained her sudden meditation on a relationship with an absent friend. The second half of the conversation, the reflection on this story, depended on the content of the initial narrative and her expanded awareness of unnoticed aspects of her experience.

Imagery, Metaphor, and Symbol

Frequently, in the spiritual-direction conversation, the directee shares an experience of God. While directees may find the words and concepts to describe the sensory, affective, and cognitive changes that result from these religious experiences, they may find these sacred tales quite difficult to tell. Because of their preconceptual aspects, directees have to rely on imagery, metaphor, and symbol to share them. They will describe a spiritual reality in terms of other experienced realities using metaphoric language to express themselves. As Kathleen Fischer says, "Religious feeling often stretches and transcends the limits of ordinary language; it must speak of the ineffable in symbol and paradox."[44]

The words—imagery, metaphor, and symbol—have a variety of meanings in different contexts. Here we are using the word *image* in two distinctly different ways: from a psychological perspective, to refer to the representation of a person, object, or scene in one's imagination; and in a linguistic perspective, to refer to a verbal evocation of an object known from experience, and its intended and suggested meanings and overtone related to a second object.

The role of imagery in the spiritual-direction conversation relates to the kinds of religious experience a particular directee may have. For instance, some people regularly pray by using the classic method of Ignatian contemplation. In this form of prayer, the person uses the imagination to reconstruct the particular details of a gospel story or an event in Christ's life and place themselves in this scene.[45] In this case, the images that arise in the prayer are the medium of the person's religious experience, and thus correspond to the first definition of the term *image*. One cannot separate the imaging from the experience; the person's imagination mediates God's presence in the image and an affective quality of response is also imaged.

Mary's story in chapter 1 suggests this kind of prayer. On the second day of the retreat she began her prayer with an image of the crucifixion and described the intensity of the pain that she brought to the scene.

> The one event in Christ's life that could bear the weight of how I felt was the crucifixion. Prayer that day began in tears, darkness, and silence. Then the

image of Christ crucified began to take on much the same expression and scars my shattered face had. I came to know that my pain was his pain and his pain was mine. Scars that were bleeding on his face were also bleeding on mine, yet his eyes revealed a great capacity for love and constant hope. In his torn, weeping, and rejected state he embraced me. I became still, and dwelt waiting, for I felt I had nothing else. I began to abandon my own being and really trust in God.[46]

Later the same day she describes how she again used this image. She identified with it and, through it, felt touched by grace. Most important, through her experience of Jesus being with her in her pain, she no longer felt isolated in her hurt and gained strength to bear it.

In spiritual direction, a story of such an imaged prayer experience will encompass what the person saw, felt, understood, said, and did. A dialogue may spontaneously emerge between the Christ figure and the one praying; also, images not in the scripture text that served as a starting point may unfold. In subsequent prayer experiences, the directee may return to the imaged scene, as Mary did, and continue to let it unfold.[47] Thus an imaged scene becomes the medium of the directee's ongoing encounter with God.[48]

We can also describe a contemplative experience of God that typically occurs without words, concepts, or images, only by using images or metaphoric language.[49] Some frequently occurring metaphors derive from the experience of darkness and light, especially the kind of light that is experienced as blinding and thus producing darkness. Gregory of Nyssa, Pseudo-Dionysius, John of the Cross, and the anonymous author of *The Cloud of Unknowing* all draw on this metaphor in their characteristically apophatic mysticism.[50] Another set of metaphors comes from the experience of waking and sleeping, forgetfulness and oblivion.[51] Yet a third set of metaphors, describing other aspects of the experience, is drawn from a love relationship between two people.[52]

Imagery in the spiritual-direction conversation also frequently arises from the director's attempt to articulate an experience a directee is trying to describe. If apt images are found, the experience becomes vivid and focused for the directee. Carol Eckerman describes the way both words and images "emerge" in the spiritual-direction conversation. She writes: "These words were emergents, gifts, rather than grasping tools. Further, multi-sensory images that embodied the essence of experiences sometimes emerged first, before words. Words might emerge later to name the image, to reflect further on its meaning, or to connect the image with the words of others."[53] Eckerman notices that images arise in her in response to her directees' stories. She then puts into words her image for the directee's situation—in one instance, a solid stone wall separating the woman from something unseen; in another, an image of a "vividly bright ball of light scattering rays in all directions." In both instances, her directees adopted these emergent images for themselves, frequently referring to the "ball of light" or the "stone wall" in later sessions.[54]

The novelist Amy Tan states in her memoir: "I loved metaphors and used them before I knew what the word meant. I thought of metaphors as secret passageways that took me to hidden rooms in my heart, and my memory as the dreamy part of myself that lived in another world."[55] The way we use metaphors often reveals the hidden rooms of our hearts, opening new worlds of possible meaning as we struggle to articulate that which is either only partially understood or so ephemeral it is hard to put into words.

Novelist John Updike described such an experience. Updike awoke from sleep in Florence, feeling "fearful and adrift, nearing my life's end, a wide-awake mote in an alien, sleeping city," in a lonely and alienated emotional state that had bothered him for some time. But it suddenly changed and he described the incident that changed it:

> But then, getting up to go to the bathroom, I became
> aware of a noise, a rustling all around me, and then
> thunder's blanketing boom, repeated. I went to the

window....While I watched, the rain intensified, rattling on tile roofs near and far; it looked like rods of metal in the floodlight that illumined part of the great—the world's greatest, pre-steel—red-tiled dome. Lightning. Hectic gusts. The rain was furious. I was not alone in the universe. The rippling rods of rain drove down upon the vertical beam of light at the base of the Duomo as if to demolish it; but the pillar of light burned on, and the hulking old church crouched like a stoic mute dragon, and the thick tiles and gurgling gutters around me withstood the soaking, the thunder, the shuddering flashes. I was filled with a glad sense of exterior activity. My burden of being was being shared. God was at work—at ease, even, in this nocturnal Florentine commotion, this heavenly wrath and architectural defiance, this Jacobean wrestle. My wife woke up, admired the solemn tempest with me, and went back to bed. I lay down beside her and fell asleep amid the comforting, busy, self-careless drumming. All this felt like a transaction, a rescue, and answered prayer.[56]

It helps that Updike was a very fine writer! However, the shift he described in his felt sense of himself in the universe is remarkable. The passage begins with his feeling like "a wide-awake mote in an alien city." He was restless, unable to sleep, feeling alone and insignificant, a mere speck, despite his wife sleeping beside him. The rain looked like "rods of metal." The rain was *furious*. He evoked a hectic, loud, chaotic storm. His emotional response to this potentially angry, destructive power was consolation.

It is as if God was speaking to him in the storm. He wrote, *"I was not alone."* Despite the threatening words of "as if to demolish" the cathedral, the lightning became a "pillar of light" such as led the Israelites by night. This potentially destructive tempest filled him with a "glad sense of exterior activity." He built on the initial feeling of "not alone": "My burden was being shared." "God was at work, at ease," in all this chaos. Updike is sufficiently comforted by the ferocious storm to fall asleep beside his wife. "All this felt like a transaction, a rescue, and answered prayer." He had been restored to the felt connection with God that he so desired.

This reliance on metaphorical expression to describe experience is neither affectively neutral nor without implications for behavior. When metaphorical images function as symbols,

> they speak to us existentially and find an echo in the inarticulate depths of our psyches. Such images communicate through their evocative power. They convey a latent meaning that is apprehended in a nonconceptual, even a subliminal way. Symbols transform the horizons of our lives, integrate our perceptions of reality, alter our scale of values, reorient our loyalties, attachments, and aspirations in a manner far exceeding the powers of abstract conceptual thought....They suggest attitudes and courses of action; they intensify confidence and devotion.[57]

We see this in Updike's description. He was reoriented to a reliable relationship with God who answered his prayers, who rescued him as the psalmist promises, and who was engaged in a "transaction" with him, ensuring him he was not alone. From feeling alone in an alien city, Updike relaxed into sleep next to his wife, reassured his prayers had been answered. Updike worked his way into the meaning and significance of this "transaction" in and through the tempest without an interlocutor. In spiritual direction, his spiritual director would have listened to his account and lingered with its unfolding revelatory qualities.

Literary critic Philip Wheelwright characterizes symbols by their permanence and stability, their rootedness in the cosmos, and their multivalence of meaning.[58] In this sense, the crucifixion could become a symbol for Mary of how Christ is present to her in her pain and offers her love and hope in the midst of it. Her image of the masked face of Christ being torn into bits and pieces mirrors her feelings about the damage done to her face by her divorce. So it is a multivalent Christian image, but also very personal to her in the way it emerged in her prayer.

By uncovering the latent meanings and logical implications of the images and symbols emerging in the spiritual-direction conversation, we glimpse the plot and affective attitudes implicit in this language. We often say more than we fully grasp when such feeling words and images pour out of our mouths. Examining the dominant symbols and patterns of imagery with people in direction gives them access to what they already know about themselves in some vague way. It had never been made explicit to Mary in direction, for example, how the particular landscapes in which she chose to pray mirrored the interior movement of the retreat. In narrative terms, the symbolism of the setting was implicitly affecting her during the retreat. She began by hiding in the rocks, in a cave overhung with growth, and gradually emerged into a night garden of delight. Finally, she moved into expansive open spaces. The geographical settings mirrored her emotional movement from isolation to embrace, from hurt to comfort, from fear to trust. Unconsciously or semiconsciously, Mary's states of feelings influenced where she chose to pray. In this case, Mary was not reporting an imaged scene, but was symbolically relating to the landscapes available near the retreat house as sensate images through which she related to God. She was enacting her relationship with God in the landscape.

A director can reinforce these symbols, intensify their effects on the person, change them by suggesting alternative scenarios or attitudes that the person might want to entertain toward events, or ignore them. In Mary's case, if images of the crucifixion had suggested being self-absorbed or being overwhelmed by her pain, the director might have tried to support her with an alternative image that would lead toward hope and strength. To suggest an alternative image can sometimes lessen the grip of a negative image and the attitude it embodies. In Updike's case, a director would most likely reinforce his emotional sense of moving from feeling isolated, to sharing his burden with God, to continuing the prayer, the transaction.

Paying attention to a person's images and symbols is rather delicate. It involves both an interpretive process that seeks to understand what a particular symbol means for this person and a process of discriminating between images that may help or harm a person's spiritual development. One can discern the helpfulness of images by "playing out" the possibilities of an image or symbol, and on the basis of that exploration, judging whether it is a helpful way of shaping thought, action, and feeling.[59]

In addition to playing out the possibilities in the images and symbols, directors should also explore the personal meaning of some symbols in order to understand their meaning and associations for the directee. Even symbols that appear to be archetypal—those carrying very similar meanings for many people—can become personalized.[60] Being submerged in water, for instance, has different associations for a person who has nearly drowned and for a proficient body-surfer.[61] In Sam's case, the small wooden puppet he recognizes as Pinocchio does not imply deception, but rather something not to be afraid of.

The way people in spiritual direction express themselves through symbols and images varies depending on the role of symbol and image in their actual religious experience. Each person has a unique pattern of images and symbols that they use to communicate experiences. Sensitive direction requires the director to invite sufficient elaboration of the significant key images or symbols to ensure the possibility of grasping their meanings.

Questions for Further Reflection

1. In what sense is telling a story a way of knowing?

2. How do you connect the sense of yourself over time and the story you tell yourself about yourself?

3. How is your story influenced by others and your religious culture?

4. What are your stories about yourself and your experience of God like?

5. In what ways do you experience God in and through images in your prayer?

6. What images or metaphors do you rely on to talk about your relationship with God?

Chapter Four
It Matters How We Tell the Story

It matters how we tell the story of our graced experience. Among the important benefits of the directee's storytelling is our narrative construction of identity. This understanding of the development of the autobiographical self and its dependence on language has been explored many times in the last twenty years in the context of postmodernism across disciplines. This narrative construction of identity is frequently based on an elaboration of an extended "metaphor of the self,"[1] and, insofar as directees recount significant episodes from their life stories, these key symbols of the self will emerge in the conversation in important ways. It is essential for directors to listen for the primary metaphors of the self of each directee because they continue to shape the directee's story in implicit ways on an ongoing basis.

Among the most important benefits of the directee's storytelling in spiritual direction is the opportunity to tell his or her life story to a receptive and interactive listener. Because this is an ongoing relationship, directees share very profound individual experiences of grace. The ongoing narrative opportunity also helps them experience a sense of personal continuity over time that they are creating, maintaining, and changing in their narrative construction of identity. The story that emerges in spiritual direction encompasses the person's spiritual identity.

In North American and European cultures, the realm of spiritual phenomena is usually restricted to the private self. Spiritual direction invites a directee to tell his or her life story, which often includes very rich spiritual experiences that he or she may never have shared before. This provides the opportunity to integrate these more deeply into a spiritual autobiography. When directees begin to bring their stories of religious experience, their denominational faith stories, their cultural and professional stories, and their identity stories into conscious dialogue with one another, they may discover both harmony and conflict among these various stories of the self. This can lead to a fruitful discernment among stories.

Most significant experiences challenge a person to find language that adequately represents the event. Directees have the opportunity to retell key stories until they can adequately assimilate their significance and implications sufficiently enough to act on them. Such storytelling tends to establish an attitude toward God and others, to make the directee more sensitive to God's activity in his or her life, and, in some cases, to precipitate a moral struggle requiring changes in lifestyle or behavior. In addition, the director's response to these stories can enhance the directee's appropriation of them. The director can invite elaboration of a story, collaborate with the directee in interpreting it, and analyze some of its features. As a result, the directee often more fully appreciates the richness and depth of his or her story and assumes more authority for actions and decisions.

Metaphors of the Self

A written autobiography is always, regardless of its imagined audience, an exercise of selection and patterned arrangement, usually organized around a central metaphor of the self that lends coherence to the story. The Cistercian Thomas Merton adopted Dante's theme of the journey up "the seven storey mountain"[2] as his central constellating metaphor. Contemporary writer Anne Lamott described her faith journey as leaping from one lily pad to another.[3] Carmelite Thérèse of Lisieux used the image of a little white flower as a metaphor for the way she understood herself; she returned several times to this image in her autobiography, *Story of a Soul*.[4] All these metaphors for the self constellate into a theme about the self, as well as imply a plot line.

Like these literary autobiographers, directees rely on key metaphors to convey a sense of the self-God relationship. For example, Krista, during a sabbatical year of healing from burnout, received in prayer and from nature two key images that foreshadowed her healing and suggested progressive stages of her intimacy with Jesus. Krista says:

> [Spiritual direction] early [in the year] was centered on self and on my woundedness. Sometimes I was "thrown" from recent wounds to those of my childhood. This was heightened because I began the program on my father's anniversary [of death] and because a tree just outside the door had a "wound" that oozed sap. This tree could not be avoided. No matter how hard I tried to turn away, still it "caught" me. Somehow this connected very deeply with a wound in the core of my being.

During the first part of her sabbatical, she could pray only in nature. The tree with its oozing wound became a metaphor for her wounded self. Although the tree was obviously wounded, the wound could heal. The healing plot began to unfold. Just being in the woodlands nurtured her. As she began to add a nightly reflection on her day emphasizing gratitude, she was still hesitant about reestablishing a "duty-bound" routine of prayer. She turned inside "seeking the truth within, the God of my heart." At that time, she says:

> I had an image of Jesus standing at the door knocking. He was left standing for quite some time, then I opened the door but left him outside. This continued for months, and it was very healthy as we could chatter at each other, one on either side of the door,

without having to look each other in the eye. I was very comfortable with this safe relationship.

In Krista's ongoing spiritual direction, this image of Jesus outside her door emerged in her prayer. An image, such as this one, changes and evolves in both predictable and often surprising ways. Such images suggest possible plot lines. These plot-bearing images, like metaphors of the self, emerge from external reality, from internal imaginative prayer, or from the spiritual-direction conversation itself. Krista's images suggest she requires time both for healing and for deepening intimacy with Jesus. Will Krista open the door? Only time will tell. In the oral autobiographical narrative in spiritual direction, these metaphors of the self and plot-bearing images may be more varied than in the more controlled literary form.

Narrative Construction of Identity

Both individuals and communities construct their identities through narrative.[5] Individuals who belong to communities weave their own identity narratives in relationship to the community's stories. The identity of a self or a community is literally embedded in and sustained by the stories each tells about who it is. The story maintains a sense of continuity through time and symbolically interprets the whole history of the self or the community through certain key events. Story becomes the mode for expressing enduring values and meanings.[6] A narrative approach to spiritual direction that pays attention to the story is, necessarily, concerned with the directee's narrative of identity.

Personal identity involves three interrelated factors:

1. the persistence of the self through time,
2. one's character (the kind of person one is becoming), and

3. the process of interpretation that depends upon memory.[7]

We construct an identity through an ongoing activity of consciousness that coherently holds together these three elements in some meaningful pattern.[8] Narrative provides a structure for this activity by symbolically allowing us to interpret the whole of a person's history through a few characteristic events. Theologian George Stroup perceptively discusses this relationship between narrative and personal identity.

> It is no accident that when they are asked to identify themselves most people recite a narrative or story....Often these narratives are simple and brief and contain only basic data, such as date and place of birth, vocation, family, etc. But with only a little probing it quickly becomes apparent that every person's identity narrative is far more subtle and complex than it first appears. In an individual's identity narrative, what we might refer to as a person's "autobiography," certain events are lifted out of that person's history and given primary importance for the interpretation and understanding of the whole....A person's identity, therefore, is an interpretation of personal history in which the meaning of the whole and hence the identity of the self is constructed on the foundation of a few basic events and the symbols and concepts used to interpret them.[9]

Contemporary autobiographical theory takes into account some of the new understandings of the self emerging from postmodernism as well as from developmental psychology and neuroscience. Paul John Eakin describes these issues under the theme of "registers of the self."[10] Through this category he answers the question, "which self is speaking in the "I" of autobiographical discourse?" A second and related question is how to integrate our bodies, brains, and our sense of self. The autobiographical "I" is a linguistic self. This idea has led some postmodernists to conclude that our identities are nothing more than linguistic creations.[11] Both personality theorists and neuroscientists point to multiple dimensions of the self, which are not entirely dependent on language, that also contribute to our sense of self.[12]

Cognitive psychologist Ulric Neisser describes five kinds of self-knowledge[13] that the autobiographical self integrates into its sense of self. Usually not experienced as separate and distinct, all five "selves" exhibit some degree of continuity over time, and so contribute to the universal experience of the continuity of the self. Neisser's five selves are:

1. The *ecological self* is the self as perceived with respect to the physical environment: "I" am the person here in this place, engaged in this particular activity. This self is present in infancy.
2. The *interpersonal self*, which appears from earliest infancy just as the ecological self does, is identified by species-specific signals of emotional rapport and communication: "I" am the person who is engaged, here, in this particular human interchange.
3. The *extended self* is based primarily on our personal memories and anticipations: "I" am the person who had certain specific experiences, and who regularly engages in certain specific and familiar routines. By the age of three, children are aware of themselves "as existing outside the present moment, and hence of the extended self."
4. The *private self* appears when children first notice that some of their experiences are not directly shared with other people: "I" am, in principle, the only person who can feel this unique and particular pain. Although experts differ as to the emergence of this sense of privacy in developmental chronology, many studies show chil-

dren are aware of the privacy of mental life before the age of five.

5. The *conceptual self* or self-concept draws its meaning from the network of assumptions and theories in which it is embedded, just as all other concepts do. Some of those theories concern social roles (husband, professor, American); some postulate more or less hypothetical internal entities (the soul, the unconscious mind, mental energy, the brain, the liver); and some establish socially significant dimensions of difference (intelligence, attractiveness, wealth). There is a remarkable variety of what people believe about themselves, and not all of it is true.[14]

I hope it is immediately clear that the autobiographical "I" who tells a sacred tale in spiritual direction primarily fashions a story from the perspective of the extended self, the private self, and the conceptual self. Internal self-representations appear only in these three selves—by contrast to the ecological self, which is directly perceived.[15] In these registers of the self, we find the confluence of the temporal dimension of self, its reflection on agency and events, and the capacity to choose to disclose unique personal experience. The extended and private selves produce identity narratives—in and through the available conceptual self—that are coded in myth, theories, religion, and philosophy.

The narrative story of identity is told by the organizing ego-consciousness of the person. Dan P. McAdams says the "I" is involved in "selfing" the "me." "I" am telling the story of "me," who becomes a character in my story. Contrary to some postmodernists, McAdams has shown that identity narratives show remarkable continuity in time, although they also evolve and develop. Identity narratives maintain stable features, while they also incorporate change over time in the sense of self. Specifically, the areas of continuity McAdams found were the level of narrative complexity and a positive

emotional tone. The themes of agency and growth orientation were also significant in their continuity. The greatest
amount of change occurred in the areas of greater levels of
emotional nuance and self-differentiation and greater understanding of their own personal development.[16] From a developmental perspective, this "selfing" process is what the ego
does, and one expects development toward greater complexity over time.

Neisser's pre-linguistic, pre-reflexive ecological and
interpersonal selves point to a sense of self firmly anchored
in our bodies. According to Antonio Damasio, "The 'neural
basis' for the self resides with the continuous reactivation of
at least two key sets of representations: one set concerns representations of key events in an individual's autobiography
and the other consists of representations of body states."[17]
Damasio distinguishes between the core self and the autobiographical self. We are conscious of this core self, which is
both prior to the autobiographical self and which remains
even if the autobiographical self is compromised by neuro-
logical injuries. This autobiographical self requires the presence of a core self and the mechanism of core consciousness
so that activation of its memories can generate core consciousness.[18] Even more importantly, Damasio says that the
autobiographical self does not depend on language. It can tell
a "story" with images or representations alone. Most of the
time for most of us, these representations are in the background of consciousness, although nonetheless continuous.
It is this sense of our body-selves that we consult when
someone asks what we are feeling in the present moment.

Although we could never remain conscious of all that
goes on in our bodies all the time, I believe that our ecological
selves and our interpersonal selves register religious experience, most importantly a sense of the presence of God. When
directees begin to tell a sacred tale of experiencing the presence of God, neuroscience would suggest that this is an
embodied experience. Both feelings and somatic awareness
shift when directees discover "they are not alone." They are not
imagining an experience within themselves but are actually

aware of an interpersonal divine Other affecting them. Spiritual directors can assist their directees by explicitly drawing out the "bodily knowing" of the ecological and interpersonal selves in relationship to specific experiences in prayer or in nature—experiences that are non-linguistic, but, nonetheless, are able to be noticed and appropriated. These registers of self are clearly part of our ongoing "experiencing," although they do not specify the content of a religious experience. As mystical life develops in some directees, their narratives may shift to simply describing an enduring sense of simple presence of their selves with God. But since the extended self is also always part of us, when consciousness shifts again, directees return to the current chapter of their life's narrative, which began with birth and which will end with death.

The extended and private selves also include the moral self: the character or kind of person we have become through our reflection, choices, and actions. We choose to tell and enact a certain kind of story with our lives, and we tend to tell ourselves that same story in our inner self-talk. These stories offer us a sense of prediction and some measure of control over our lives. If our story is a story of victimization or of "things just happening" without our consent or participation, we have not yet become conscious of ourselves as storytellers, as having the capacity to authorize our lives, change our minds and our behaviors, and create another story or chapter in our lives. Spiritual direction is a privileged narrative situation that invites reflection on, and revision or repair of, our stories, especially in a faith context. For instance, one directee's story of discovering that God was with her even when she felt lonely and alone as a child illustrates such revision and repair. After this discovery of the divine Presence in her childhood, she was able to modify her story to being accompanied by God even in her current periods of loneliness.[19] By hearing our stories when we tell them to a spiritual director, we can choose to change our stories to some degree. And as we change, our stories will also change.

In spiritual direction, the director wants to understand the person's spiritual identity, the sense of self he or she experi-

101

ences and therefore interprets as related to the divine Being. Contemporary psychological understandings of the self now assume that all selves are formed in an intersubjective context of interpersonal relationship.[20] Selves are always selves-in-relationship. In Neisser's framework, relational selves precede language. All identity narratives necessarily include our characterizations of the significant others and communities that have influenced our sense of self positively or negatively.[21]

For those who consciously relate to God in an interpersonal way, their spiritual identity is constellated around this relationship. This relationship with God is rarely explored in therapeutic contexts unless it is problematic. But in spiritual direction, the primary focus of attention is on the quality of this relationship as it unfolds consciously in the directee's life. The "story of a soul," as many historical spiritual autobiographies are envisioned, is always the story of a self being influenced in both conscious and unconscious ways by God. Being the object of God's unconditional love becomes a valuable source from which a directee derives personal dignity and significance. As this offer of love becomes conscious, directees are encouraged to respond to this love in freedom and with gratitude. In addition, their evolving spiritual identity is expected to expand to reverence the spiritual identity of others. Theologically, Christians understand that God also loves all other human beings in the same way; thus, there is necessarily a social dimension implicit in spiritual direction that includes not only the immediate relational circle of a directee, but the communities to which he or she may belong, as well as to all others about whom God is concerned.

The fact that a person's spiritual identity emerges in a dialogical process with the divine Being poses an interesting question as to who or what part of the self actually authors the narrative in spiritual direction. Psychoanalytic and personality theories seem to agree that the conscious ego constructs identity. However, the ego inevitably creates an inadequate story of the self, for it is the nature and function of the ego to repress some events. A person's inability to maintain a coherent and reasonably accurate narrative that accounts for actual personal history is a symptom of serious mental dysfunction.[22] On the other hand, psychologist C. G. Jung and his followers, such as James Hillman, give less emphasis to the deformation of the client's ego narrative and more to the story the psyche tries to tell through the images and symptoms that contest the story the ego maintains.[23] This kind of therapy aims to heal the person through eliciting stories that the ego does not totally control. These stories can contribute to changing attitudes and behaviors espoused by the ego.

Although directees may actually tell these types of psychoanalytic narratives (an inadequate story of the self or a secret story concealed in images that is produced by the unconscious in dreams) in the spiritual-direction situation, the director primarily listens for the story God is trying to tell in, through, and with the person seeking direction. John Navone and Michael Cooper assert that "human stories are implicitly coauthored with God and neighbor."[24] Theologian John S. Dunne puts it slightly differently. He describes prayer as:

> listening to God telling me the story of my journey in time....Of course it seems the opposite, I am telling the story and God is listening to me tell it. When I encounter the "real," however, as in "what does not work," then indeed it does seem God is telling the story and I am involved in an "encounter with God in the real."...If I pay attention, if I listen then to God telling me my story, I keep reshaping and elaborating the story like an epic singer who is essentially a "listening composer."...My story is a mystery to me because I am in the story....[I can ask,] "I wonder what sort of a tale we've fallen into?"...What I don't know, being in it, is how my story comes out. There is something like this in the very telling of a story. It can be made to come out in different ways.[25]

Insofar as the person is in relationship with God, God's activity will break into the narrative by causing some kind of disorganization, contradicting an absolute form of self-assertion of the ego, or emerging as some inexplicable and mysterious confusion. By attending to these intrusions, the director may be able to help directees piece together a story of God and themselves, one that is not exclusively the story of the ego. The person's ego encounters a reality that contests its dominance and its attitudes as much as, if not more so, than the psychoanalytic account of the unconscious.[26]

Theologically, the Judeo-Christian tradition believes that God acts in human history. When an individual experiences God, he or she necessarily does so within the context of his or her life story (history). Unfortunately, many people do not articulate their identity/life story narratives, even to themselves, in any comprehensive way. In large part, only those who have experienced something unusual or exceptional have engaged in such articulation.[27] For example, in the spiritual tradition, beginning with Augustine, those who wrote autobiographies in the form of confessions or religious testimonies thought of their experiences as relevant to others or received encouragement from their spiritual directors to write accounts of their spiritual lives[28] in order to teach others what they had learned experientially about prayer or the God-human relationship.

This tendency to restrict life writing to persons of exceptional talent or grace often leaves "ordinary" people with the sense that their experience is somehow insignificant or inferior. In the face of the rapid cultural changes eroding traditional values, of the increase in technologies of various kinds, and of the increased awareness of individuals and cultures that are very different from our own, many (post)modern people suffer a lack of meaning and coherence in individual human lives.[29] Betty Bergland asserts that

> autobiographies and autobiographical studies [that are] focused on ethnic groups and women have especially proliferated in the last two decades in the wake of feminist scholarship and the burgeoning field of ethnic studies. Thus, despite pro-

nouncements about the end of autobiography and postmodern challenges to traditional notions of the self, autobiographical narratives proliferate.[30]

However, even in the face of this depersonalization, the Judeo-Christian tradition affirms that each human being has worth and significance by virtue of his or her graced relationship to a personal God. There seems to be a greater need for ordinary people and especially anyone who is at all marginalized to tell their life story in an appropriate setting. Since the 1970s, there has been a movement in pastoral care and work with the elderly to encourage ordinary people to engage in some kind of "life story conversation" in order to discover the religious meaning of their lives. People tend not to "tell their story" in any great detail unless an occasion prompts them.[31] The narrative construction of identity involves interpreting and making sense of the whole of one's life by creating a meaningful configuration; without occasions for such "tellings," the life-story narrative tends to remain fragmented in consciousness and functions only implicitly in the person's activity. Consequently, many people view their lives as a series of individual events, more like a collection of snapshots than a coherent story.

Realizing how one is personally caught up in relationship with the divine Other does not and cannot happen all at once simply because of the inherent historicity of human experience. It is a gradual process that remains vulnerable to personal, cultural, and social obstacles. Personal obstacles are psychological blocks, most likely rooted in one's characteristic style of relationship with others, which one transfers to the God-human relationship. Cultural and social obstacles exist in the form of alternative identity stories that do not account for one's spiritual identity or that oppose the kind of freedom vis-à-vis culture and social groups that the spiritually mature achieve. Without an understanding of their "personal myth" (the story or stories they actually live), directees may not perceive the conflicts among the stories they are living simultaneously.[32]

Just as the emergence and solidification of a person's spiritual identity can be impeded, so, too, it can be fostered and encouraged. Historically, spiritualities are cultural and religious systems that include strategies for overcoming obstacles to spiritual development. The process of spiritual direction is one of the specific means traditionally and currently concerned with fostering "the hidden orientation or directedness towards Mystery that is present in the core of each person's being and that corresponds with his or her unique spiritual identity or calling."[33]

Spiritual direction as a narrative event offers a social opportunity for telling and interpreting stories of religious experience, which are essentially Christian identity narratives. People seeking direction narrate their lives in the light of their personal experience of God, their shared convictions with the larger community of faith, and their vision of the people they are becoming. The interpersonal setting of this narrative occasion lends social reality and significance to experiences that contemporary American culture privatizes. This privatization of religious experience—and the spiritual identity emerging from it—discourages its social articulation and the social action it requires in response. By providing an arena for exploring these experiences through recounting and then discussing them in the light of a shared community of faith, spiritual direction supports and encourages the directee in attending to this dimension of reality and in responding to it.

Effects of Narrative Activity

A narrative approach to spiritual direction accomplishes more than fostering the emergence in narrative of a person's spiritual identity:

1. The directee's narrative activity establishes the person's pervasive attitude toward God and other people.

   2. It enables the person to relive religiously signif-
       icant experience with greater appreciation for
       God's activity in his or her life.
   3. It engenders an ongoing sensitivity to God's
       activity.
   4. It frequently precipitates moral struggle in re-
       sponse to religiously significant experience.

A director sensitive to the narrative representation of experience recognizes that the directee will often need to tell key
experiences more than once in order to adequately express
and assimilate them into the life story narrative. The director
can enhance the directee's appropriation of his or her life
experience through elaboration, interpretation, or analysis of
the directee's narrative.

Retelling Key Stories

    People tend to tell and retell a single story numerous
times. Why? First, multiple repetitions of an important story
constitute attempts to express what happened and to explore
its meaning for the narrator. Significant and complex experiences do not yield their meaning in one narration. Second,
experiences that challenge the directee's assumptions or previous construction of identity require the person to reconstruct his or her life story in the light of this new experience.
The following provides an example of a story that will likely
go through several retellings:

> Several years ago a group of computer salesmen
> from Milwaukee went to a regional sales convention
> in Chicago. They assured their wives that they
> would be home in plenty of time for dinner. But
> with one thing or another the meeting ran overtime
> so the men had to race to the station, tickets in
> hand. As they barreled through the terminal, one
> man [the one telling this story] inadvertently kicked
> over a table supporting a basket of apples. Without
> stopping they all reached the train and boarded it

with a sigh of relief. All but one. He paused, got in touch with his feelings, and experienced a twinge of compunction for the boy whose apple stand had been overturned. He waved goodbye to his companions and returned to the terminal. He was glad he did. The ten-year-old boy was blind.

The salesman gathered up the apples and noticed that several of them were bruised. He reached into his wallet and said to the boy, "Here, please take this ten dollars for the damage we did. I hope it didn't spoil your day." As he started to walk away the bewildered boy called after him, "Are you Jesus?"

He stopped in his tracks and wondered.[34]

Were the computer salesman to tell this story in spiritual direction, he would most likely not share a polished narrative. He might try to describe this experience of mystery, one that requires something of him after this event. He might focus on his feelings about the event: What prompted him to return to the terminal? How did the blind boy's question affect him? Is he like Jesus in his life? How might he have been running too fast? In what sense is *he* blind? The man might need multiple retellings to understand the experience in all its complexity and richness. These retellings do not strive for narrative artistry but for a satisfactory narrative interpretation of the experience. Minimally, this interpretation includes both what happened and what it means to the narrator from the perspective of the present.[35] The man might return to the story until he can decide concretely what he needs to change in his life in order to live out the implications of this experience. Whenever someone touches the mystery of human existence or the Mystery at the source of one's very being, a facile, single narration of the experience does not suffice to render all of its richness.

If the salesman assimilates the effects of this experience through his storytelling, he might begin to live and to tell his life story with a different emphasis. He might notice ways he does not act like the kind of person he wishes to become. Or he might choose to reflect on his life and notice when and how he ran so fast that he hurt other people. This narrative reinterpretation of the "story" he has been living (i.e., "running too fast") allows him to view his past behavior from a new perspective. The new experience calls him to assess a story he might have named "The Front-Runner Salesman" and to rename or reinterpret that story as "The Christian Who Was Blind to What Really Matters." This incident seems to require some form of conversion, a change in his life story.[36] However, by contrast, the man might simply incorporate an experience that was more typical for him as one more important event he uses to organize his identity-narrative.

Opal, a spiritual director-in-training, describes the gradually unfolding levels of insight that occurred through repeated retellings of an incident that happened to her in class.

> I told this story [about the incident] to a variety of people who hear me with ears based on the roles they play in my life. I am sure I told the story differently or accented different parts of it with each person. Because it was a recent event, I was able to tell it in a concrete fashion, giving as many details as possible. As I retold it, I began to develop levels of understanding. Each retelling was a layer with a different insight attached to it—as shells and fossils imbedded in sedimentary rock. The wisdom coming as a result of the retelling was unearthed in the shells and fossils. Looking at John Shea's categories of religious experience, my fossils and shells were enough to fill a bell jar! I most resonated with the questions, Why am I bringing this up now? Why is my experience of [this incident] important now?

Effects of Narration on the Directee

In spiritual direction, people frequently tell stories about religiously significant experiences. These stories deal either directly with God or with other people and life experiences illumined by God's presence. Spiritual direction fosters sensitivity to this dimension of life experience by being open to these stories. The directee's narration of these stories produces three major effects, which are rooted in the nature of narrative itself.

First, in creating religiously significant narratives, the narrator reenters the feelings and events in a way that moves beyond merely noting patterns or talking analytically about the experience. Storytelling re-creates the experience for both the narrator and the audience with emotional power. This provides an opportunity for the storyteller to appreciate the experience more fully and to reenter the presence of the mysterious Other originally encountered in the experience. For instance, each time the salesman tells his story and repeats the boy's question, he finds that it addresses him again on an emotional level.

Second, relating the experience establishes the narrator's pervasive attitude and outlook concerning either God or life lived in relationship to God. The narrator tells the story by using words to convey emotion and tone. The point of view is sometimes crystallized in a pithy sentence in which the narrator adds to the story what he or she got out of it. These attitudes and perspectives emerge from the narrative process itself and may or may not match the attitudes and point of view the person had *during* the experience. For instance, in Sam's case—the seminarian in chapter 1 who was discerning whether or not to be ordained—he described an experience of being called as "having lost it." These words carried his subsequent attitude of embarrassment more accurately than his original feeling of awe and love. And if he had continued to tell this story emphasizing the embarrassment, he might have established embarrassment as his pervasive attitude about this experience.

Emerging from the first two effects is a third: that reliving the experience and establishing one's attitude and point of view "engenders a particular sensitivity and precipitates certain moral conflicts."[37] The computer salesman's experience with the apple seller made him increasingly aware of attitudes and behaviors about which he had been oblivious. He was sensitive enough to his own feelings that, when he got on the train, he knew something wasn't quite right. When he responded to that feeling by returning to the terminal, the subsequent events provoked further awareness and demands. If he tells and retells this story, he will increase his sensitivity to the invitation to become more like a Jesus kind of person. This pull toward discipleship will remain alive in his heart and imagination. He will reinforce the initial moral response he felt during the incident to make restitution for the damage he had caused, and thus the storied event can precipitate a new moral struggle to change his future behavior. Telling and retelling the story thus keeps the tension of this future-oriented demand present in his consciousness as he seeks to live out the meaning the experience disclosed.

These three effects—reliving the experience, establishing attitudes and point of view, and fostering sensitivity and moral struggle—flow from telling and retelling such a story and are distinct from the listener's/audience's response. The person explores the experience and its meaning by telling this tale and continues to tell and retell it as a way of appropriating it into his or life story and acting on its significance.

In many of these tellings, the audience may be fairly passive. The narrator tries out a way of expressing the experience and its personal meaning in each telling. Some audiences could, however, contest this narrator's sense of significance. For instance, the other salesmen, feeling a twinge of guilt, might not want to hear about the blind boy and might even ridicule the man for going back to the terminal. Other people might deny the religious significance of the story and dismiss it as pure coincidence. Such responses would affect how the narrator tells his story in the future and might even discourage him from continuing to retell it at all. Spiritual direction, with its special interest in religiously significant experiences, affords a privileged opportunity for rendering these experiences into a narrative that can be received with reverence and sensitivity.

The Director's Response

The director can respond to a directee's narrative in a number of ways. Obviously, the first and most crucial response consists in attentive listening. The willingness to listen to another articulate the religious dimension of his or her experience proves necessary for the above effects on the narrator to occur at all. The spiritual-direction situation is, however, characteristically interactive; the director only rarely acts as a passive auditor.

In a narrative approach to direction, the director responds to the directee's story in ways that respect the actual narrative, as well as use theological, scriptural, psychological, and spiritual frames of reference. These additional frames of reference can be discovered within the narrative itself and used to thematize the particular experiences related in the story. Following the directee's narrative clues, the director responds in these ways:

- Discerns growth and development of the directee in the narrative
- Listens attentively to the narrative
- Elicits further elaboration of narrative detail or additional stories
- Analyzes and comments on the plot, tone of voice, image patterns, affects, conflicts, atmosphere, or character development
- Interprets this narrative in relationship to the directee's religious and cultural traditions

This attention to narrative clues allows the director to offer a nonjudgmental response to the narrative by focusing on what is "there." The director's response highlights or brings forward different facets of the narrative and allows for exploration of their implications with the directee.

Discerning

Discernment of Spirits

Far from being without motive, spiritual direction aims to encourage the directee's recognition of and response to God's direction in the unique circumstances of his or her life. Accomplishing this goal presupposes the director's experiential and general knowledge of the spiritual life and a consequent prudential ability to co-discern with the directee his or her spiritual orientation. This assessment of a directee's general spiritual orientation figures among the first discernments a director needs to make, according to Ignatius's "Rules for the Discernment of Spirits" in the *Spiritual Exercises*. In these guidelines, Ignatius describes two types of people: one group is basically oriented toward an increasingly God-filled life, which they demonstrate by the overall quality of their lives and the effects of their activity; the other group is dominated by a tendency that leads away from God and whose activity proves destructive for themselves and others.[38] In addition to this general orientation, people also discover they can be mistaken about experiences that promise to go in a certain direction but in actuality fail to do so. Discernment, then, involves assessing how specific actions or events relate to an individual's general direction.

This intention to foster an orientation toward the good and toward God guides the director in responding to narratives offered in spiritual direction. The director listens for details that indicate whether the person is generally maturing or regressing in relationship to God and responds in a way that helps the directee assess the progressive or regressive effect of particular experiences or choices upon this relationship. As the directee narrates various events of religious significance, the director's response to that narrative can enable the directee to grow in self-knowledge, which constitutes one of the fundamental conditions for maturing in the spiritual life.[39]

Charles, a middle-aged priest on retreat, described this interaction with his director:

I told my retreat director that I had a desire to grow in affective intimacy with Jesus. Although the affective aspect of my prayer had from time to time been strong or had at least occasionally powerfully punctuated my prayer, I mentioned that in general I had veered toward a more intellectual engagement with God. Afterward, I spent time with a passage from the gospel, and, when I met with my director the next day, I began reading to him line after line from my notes, rapidly sharing insight after insight. In many ways each of my frenetic observations was aimed at moving from the head to the heart. When I got to the line, "trying to operate without words," he stopped me and said, "Charles, go back and read that line again." It wasn't until then that I realized I had documented my failure to do that which I desired. In choosing what to tell, what I told, and in considering the message I had wanted to communicate, I had no idea that latent in that story was a message I needed to hear. Had I not subjected myself to the discipline of spiritual direction, I may never have heard it. In other circumstances when I tell a story, I already have the message. In direction when I tell a story, I get one, and the director with the grace of God is essential.

Discernment of Stories

Spiritual direction as a narrative process actively invites both telling the sacred tale and paying close attention to the potentially incompatible stories directees may be trying to live. In ongoing spiritual direction, during every session directees express their inner autobiographical activity, modified by the assumptions made about both the director's receptivity to this story and its relevance to the story of self and God together. This is a relational form of autobiography recently receiving more literary critical attention.[40] The spiritual-direction process welcomes the directee's unique narrative. Every directee has already been encoded with a plethora of possible mythic patterns. In the postmodern context, the admission of multiple points of view and horizons of experience has radically expanded these narrative possibilities. When directees hear themselves telling their unique and particular stories that include gender, ethnicity, family history, subculture, sexual orientation, faith tradition, particular communities, and natural environment, they become more aware of the story they are living. These stories may contain hidden conflicts and significant value differences among the various subplots and story lines. Tad Dunne coined the phrase *discernment of stories* to describe an important element of spiritual direction by examining the many story lines of directees' lives in relationship to one another.[41]

Directees absorb stories from films; from celebrities; from confessional talk shows on every imaginable subject; from the plots of sitcoms, soap operas, and other television shows; from many written forms of personal narratives; and from cultural templates. These stories often define success in terms of financial status; they define self-worth in terms of sexual attraction or display; they define the use of force in terms of the only way to resolve conflict; they define the violation of human rights and civil liberties in terms of a necessity to calm fear. These stories live inside us right along with the stories of our faith, with the story of Jesus, and with the parabolic stories Jesus told to draw us toward God's desires for us.

Discernment of stories suggests that a major function of spiritual direction regarding narratives is to recognize when two or more plots that a directee is trying to live simultaneously are in conflict in fundamental ways. Dunne believes that these myths or tropes of our culture restrict our imaginations, our desires, and, consequently, our actions. The discernment of stories demands "a readiness to ask whether our desires may be overly restricted by a kind of myth—the myth, say, that the Bible contains the only truths necessary; or that life is ultimately tragic, or paradoxical, or threatening, or fertile, or complex, or simple, and so on. Each such myth, or story, limits the field of possible desires."[42]

115

This discernment of stories is not limited to the exploration of conflicts between secular and sacred stories. It often involves conflicts among different, competing forms of the Christian story itself, to say nothing of all the other ways of being religious we may encounter in spiritual direction today. Some versions of the Catholic Christian tradition continue to severely limit the possible faith stories that women, gays, lesbians, and members of many ethnic groups—who are all also members of the church—might enact. The ideological conflicts over the interpretation of Vatican II play out in multiple ways in the faith stories of laity, religious, and clergy alike. They determine how we construe our "roles" within the ecclesial community.

Part of Tad Dunne's remedy for directees caught in a limiting story is the ability to glimpse an alternative possibility. Dunne suggests that "the ability to distinguish between reliable and unreliable stories depends on how educated we are in alternative stories."[43] When directees can imagine an alternative pattern or possibility, they can often create a new story that is more adequate than the original, unreflective one. We are very familiar with this critical approach to the manifest narrative in psychoanalysis or other forms of therapy. Directors can assist their directees by inviting them to imagine an alternative story or by suggesting more than one alternative plot to stimulate directees' creative resolutions of these story lines in partnership with God.

Listening

The director can facilitate the directee's self-knowledge and growing God-awareness by listening in a way that appreciates the efforts involved in telling a story that may prove difficult to articulate. Frequently, ordinary events mediate the experience of God, who remains in the background as almost a hidden presence that the directee nonetheless feels. The subtlety of such experiences makes them very difficult to describe. Because directees value them and yet at the same time find them difficult to articulate, they often refuse to share such experiences for fear of exposing themselves and their stories to ridicule or hostility. A director's ability to be fully present to the story of another and to encourage exploration of his or her experience may often be all the directee needs to concretize the experience sufficiently through narrative and thus receive it more fully.

The ability to listen in this enabling way often corresponds to the quality of the director's own religious experience. Directors usually need to be highly attuned to God's movement in their own lives in order to receive the mystery of God's interaction with others. This receptivity and attunement to God's presence and actions is not always conveyed in words. In the interchange between a directee who is relating a valued experience within the horizon of faith and a director who is often silent, the directee may learn to listen to the story he or she tells and to perceive what God's action has been, as well as his or her response to that action. The enabling effect upon the narrator of reverent and attentive listening has to do with the face-to-face oral process of spiritual direction. The immediacy of the relationship between the teller and the listener strongly affects storytelling as an oral event. A bond forms between the narrator and the listener-audience that is its own form of intimacy.

Kevin, a Jesuit Scholastic, described this sense of deep connection that he found in spiritual direction. After describing an insightful interchange with his retreat director, he says:

> During conversations like the one above, when I knew that insight and knowledge were being imparted to me, there would be a peaceful humming warmth in the room. In the conversation, there was a deep connection between me and the director. He was obviously receiving consolation [sensing God's presence], deeply involved in the process with a sense of wonder. I was conscious of being loved and accepted by my director, but not only by him. For me, Jesus has always been the great Teacher and the

117

Spirit, the great Guide. Looking back at that moment and others like it, I believe that Jesus was in the words, as the giver of a gift of knowledge, or perhaps in my director....The Spirit was in the warmth around us, as power. It was because of the power in the room that accompanied us that the conversation sunk into my mind and heart, giving me new ways to pray and to trust that God was with me. Since this experience and others like it in direction and elsewhere, I have come to notice that I feel God's presence as power filling a space around me.

Eliciting the "Unsaid"

In addition to the contemplative listening described above, the director may respond to a directee's narrative by inviting him or her to elaborate some aspect of it. Elaboration may be required to clarify both something in the sequence of the narrative and something about its meaning for the narrator. For example, earlier we read about Linda, the religious sister on retreat who mistook a spiritual experience to be a sexual fantasy about a friend. By eliciting details of her relationship with that friend and of what immediately preceded and followed her prayer experience, the director helped to clarify that Linda's fantasies about her friend were not the source of her sexual feelings. The expanded narrative revealed that the feelings that emerged in the prayer experience led to reverie about the friendship. In this instance, in order to understand the relationship between the prayer experience and the friendship, the director invited the story about the friendship. Often a directee will respond to a question about the meaning of an event by telling another story about an experience that occurred at some other time in his or her life. The directee recognizes that the director needs the earlier story in order to understand what the present event means. Thus, the directee interprets the present story in part by telling another story.

In addition to inviting elaboration or expansion of meaning through another story, the director may also elicit that

118

which remains "unsaid" by the narrator. According to the philosopher Martin Heidegger, it is of the very nature of articulating the truth that there is always something unsaid, something that could not be said at the time that later can be brought forward. Linda's case illustrates this principle as well. She could not describe her sexual feelings in terms of her experience of God and her response to that interaction because she thought of the two as incompatible. When the director mentioned some classical and contemporary writers in the spiritual tradition who had described and treated the relationship between the erotic and the spiritual, Linda became free to create a new narrative that more accurately represented her experience.

Not only is there an "unsaid" that cannot be articulated because of conceptual confusion or the lack of suitable categories, there is also an "unsaid" that is a part of any imaginative construction. Theologian Ray Hart says:

> For everything said, there is a particular unsaid that is essential to imaginative meaning, an unsaid that is not stipulated but rather is iconically signified. For the immediately present, denotated, delineated actuality...there is a mediate, connotated, marginal background; iconic penumbrity *is* essential to imaginative meaning and reference. For every object grasped in imaginative symbol, there is a "world" in which self and object are disclosed to each other in polysemous intercourse.[44]

Gestalt therapy developed by Frederick (Fritz) Perls made this principle imminently practical in its work. Everything in the foreground that is fully articulated has an assumed, unspoken background. For instance, if someone uses the metaphor of a sandy beach, the ocean or lake lies in the background and is implied by the beach in the foreground. Any part brought forward implies the context of the whole that lies in the background.[45] Although a spiritual director may differ much from Fritz Perls in working with this background material, a director attuned to narrative clues will sense and invite the "unsaid" into explicit awareness. This "unsaid" is not something the director knows and the directee does not. Rather, the director encourages the directee to articulate what, at some level, the directee already knows.

This example from a spiritual-direction session illustrates the point well. Ellen, a laywoman involved in justice work, was speaking about her spiritual director, Karla:

> My story of my own life was shifting significantly, but Karla always seemed more concerned with my present relationship with Jesus. At some point, my previous experience of being with Jesus alone in a boat faded from my imaginative prayer, and I began spending prayer time each morning with Jesus on dry land. Sometimes we were on a river bank; sometimes in a field; sometimes in the rocky, dusty hills of Palestine. My morning prayer time, for the first time in my life, became a precious and fundamental part of each day. It was usually an emotionally charged time as well. I was beginning to know Jesus as an intimate friend and to trust his presence even when prayer led me into tumult or deep sadness. Karla asked me when I began to feel certain of Jesus' presence.

Ellen:	During my morning prayers. Within the last couple of months.
Karla:	Is that the only time?
Ellen:	No. When I think about Jesus during the day, I feel his presence, too.
Karla:	So Jesus has been present to you for a couple of months?
Ellen:	No, that's not what I meant. I began to feel Jesus' presence a couple of months ago, but he has always been there.

Karla:	How far back in your life?
Ellen:	From the beginning. Even when I felt all alone in the world, he had to be there.

Ellen continued:

> This dialogue led me to a new consciousness of my past. Knowing that I had not endured, and am not now enduring, sad times alone, I can look at the course of my life differently. It may be more accurate to say that I can now look at my life.

Ellen knew more about herself and God than she realized. When Karla elicited what she already knew but had not really noticed, she began to create a significant reinterpretation of her spiritual identity narrative.

Finally, what a person says in an oblique way often simply goes unnoticed in the spiritual-direction conversation. Literary critic Frank Kermode labels this quality in a narrative its "secrets." He argues that within the narrative itself there exist clues or secrets that stand at odds with sequence. These secrets in some way contest the narrative coherence achieved by sequence and could be significant if attended to.[46] In spiritual direction, the director may well need to invite elaboration of this kind of "story within a story." Experiences that the directee finds difficult to talk about and yet wants to express may only be hinted at in the narrative. If the director ignores these hidden clues, the directee will not likely tell this particular story as a main episode. We see this narrative indirection, or telling a story in "code," in Sam's case when he describes his response to the ordination service in terms of having "lost it." The director's positive acceptance of his feeling of embarrassment, combined with an expressed interest in the mysterious experience Sam hinted at in his story, invited the more significant story partially hidden in the initial narrative.

There is also another kind of "secret," Frederich Buechner asserts in his memoir, *Telling Secrets*:

It is important to tell at least from time to time the secret of who we truly and fully are—even if we tell it only to ourselves—because otherwise we run the risk of losing track of who we truly and fully are and little by little come to accept instead the highly edited version which we put forth in hope that the world will find it more acceptable than the real thing. It is important to tell our secrets too because it makes it easier that way to see where we have been in our lives and where we are going....It is by entering that deep place inside us where our secrets are kept that we come perhaps closer than we do anywhere else to the One who, whether we realize it or not, is of all our secrets the most telling and the most precious we have to tell.[47]

Buechner risks telling family secrets, such as his father's alcoholism and suicide and his daughter's struggle with anorexia. Amy Tan in *The Opposite of Fate* gradually discovers family secrets such as her grandmother's suicide, which deeply affected her own life. Both writers suggest that great liberation comes from bringing these secrets into the light. Bringing such secrets (often known on some level) into spiritual direction offers directees the great relief of not being judged the less for them, as well as opens new avenues for grace. At the same time, Buechner also suggests that keeping such secrets promotes an exhausting inauthenticity.

Daniel de Roulet echoes these sentiments:

What I would like church to be like is a meeting place of authenticity, in which everyone, believer and nonbeliever alike, is acknowledged to be human and flawed and in need of a God who can do something about it—and we love one another with no strings attached....I wish that my own life, with friends and family in and outside of the church, could be one of sharing of stories about lost sons and fathers—stories where, despite the hard eclipses of life, God is always with us, and still calls us.[48]

De Roulet uses the metaphor of eclipses for life events that create such darkness or disorientation one cannot see where one is going—when one's accustomed plot is disrupted. Although some faith-sharing groups may not be able to accommodate such stories of eclipse, spiritual direction should surely be a place that can. The story we learn to tell in spiritual direction eventually requires us to tell such secrets so that they can be integrated into the rest of our stories and be brought into the light in such a way as to meet God's grace in these stories, too.

Analyzing and Commenting on Narrative Elements

In another kind of response to the directee's narrative, the director analyzes and/or comments on elements of the story, primarily by utilizing the vocabulary of literary criticism. This commentary may do any of the following: identify the plot pattern and possible outcomes; reflect back to the directee the patterns of imagery, affects, themes, motifs, tone, and atmosphere; suggest alternative plots or related images; or identify conflicts among various subplots. All of these responses are based on narrative clues provided by the directee. Frequently, comments that help the directee notice what he or she has woven into the narrative enhance his or her freedom either to maintain this story and its direction or to change some part of it. Because these responses respect the directee's freedom and honor the narrative, the directee tends to receive them as nonjudgmental and in harmony with the sacred tale being told.

The director gives primary attention to reflection on the plot, because it embodies the directee's operative theories and provides a basis for predicting possible patterns of future action. Thus the director may abstract the pattern of the plot by renaming it according to an archetypal myth or fairy tale (identifying it as comedy, tragedy, romance, satire), or by comparing it to another plot pattern available in the culture (for example, a soap opera, or a typical story of success). This analysis of plot structure may take several forms. Often simply restating the pattern in more general terms than the original story helps the narrator see his or her basic plot. Often the directee's story repeats the major plot in one form or another in several sessions with different characters and scenes. Identifying this kind of plot helps the storyteller recognize how he or she typically organizes and interprets experience.

A particular pattern, for example, seemed to organize several episodes of one woman's narrative in spiritual direction. She consistently related stories about herself in which she was somehow victimized by others' demands or in which she felt powerless. At the same time, in other scenes she exhibited a considerable amount of personal power. By describing for her the pattern found in these stories and identifying the powerlessness/powerful motif, the director helped the woman make a connection between these conflicting plots and begin to realize that she was also powerful in some situations.

This particular story also shows how a person may be living two conflicting plots simultaneously. As a woman, she had internalized much of the cultural story of female powerlessness and had internalized that script. However, she also had developed considerable personal power that she wanted to exercise without taking responsibility for it. An exploration of these contradictory attitudes toward power and the way she expressed them in her life story helped her to recognize what she was doing and begin to change her relationship to her personal power.

Following a story also entails recognizing the causal relationship between one event or attitude and the consequences that flow from it. Once a story begins to unfold, the listener (or reader) wants to know not only what happens next but also where it is going. The listener begins to project possible outcomes or consequences suggested by plot development. Although the story may not fulfill the listener's projections, sharing them with the directee may increase his or her options in concluding a particular episode.[49] Despite the outcomes suggested by the story itself, both the director and the directee may be surprised by unpredictable events (complications) that intervene and shift its entire direction.[50]

Images as well as plot sequences affect the direction of a narrative. As presented earlier, Mary was on a retreat after a bad divorce. Her experiences included many images that could have been explored in this way. For instance, twice in her narrative she described a torn or scarred face that helped her connect with Christ. First, she identified with the Christ-mask that the retreatants had made and that was then torn to pieces during the paraliturgy; in that, she felt her own face—her identity and beauty—being disfigured. Second, she recognized her scarred and bleeding face in Christ's suffering face. That enabled her to choose to pray with an image of the crucifixion.

Mary wrote the account of her retreat (which was presented in chapter 1) about three years *after* the retreat itself. Some time *still later*, I was able to interview her and there she elaborated on her ongoing reflections: "It was as if Jesus and I were one person, and I began to realize that he experienced exactly the same thing that I did. It was really as if we were one person and I would use that and pray with it. And somehow I got this insight that he knew what it was like. I felt a very physical pain, and I also got that sort of sense that he was with that pain too. So I guess the images would merge almost."[51] This identification with Jesus resulted in intimacy, support, and comfort. Mary felt understood and felt "much more hope that it would work out." Implicit in the pain of the images was some form of "resurrection" and positive resolution.

Mary also saw the image of a face emerge in a dream following her experience of God in the garden. "A young shallow girl with a flawless face had been replaced by a scarred, wrinkled woman." Mary described the true beauty and love in the woman's face, which paralleled a similar quality in the crucified Christ. Mary learned wisdom and love through her suffering. Her feminine images mirrored Christ images.

Her dream and prayer images prefigured healing and spiritual growth. Through a unique form of female suffering—rejection by her husband—she was drawn into unitive experiences with Christ crucified and with God as lover. Simultaneously, feminine images of God—the wise woman and the friend who bandages the nearly severed head—began to emerge. Both sets of images indicated the direction of Mary's growth and a subsequent revelation of the feminine in God. These images demonstrated a dynamic movement toward positive resolution to Mary's suffering even while she still felt emotionally overwhelmed by her suffering. While her spiritual director had his own approach, reflecting back this dynamic, already present in her consciousness, could have been very encouraging to her.[52]

In responding to the story, the director can reflect back different elements of it to its teller, although responding to every element in a narrative would be too much. In a particular story, the director is likely to emphasize one or another element more than others. Sometimes, rather than working with the images, the director may describe the feelings evoked by the use of language or the general tone of the narrative. At another time the director may focus on the plot; and still another time, on the atmosphere permeating the story.

The narrative atmosphere rarely receives attention in literary criticism. Literary critic Wesley Kort defines it as "an image within a narrative of possibilities and powers which lie beyond the borders of human alteration, understanding, and control....What lies beyond understanding and control is the common ground between religion and narrative."[53] The element of atmosphere allows the experience of "mystery" to enter into the narrative. Such experiences result from God's revealing God's self through ordinary life experiences, both those of limitation and of otherness.[54]

Relating the Narrative to the Tradition

In a fifth type of response to the directee's narrative, the director may explore the relationship between the story and the faith tradition in which it is rooted. The director may do this by comparing the directee's narrative with other stories in the tradition, stories either in scripture or in the lives of saintly people. If the story seems a contemporary version of the Christian story that many other people also seem to be telling, the director may expand the directee's sense of belonging to a community by making that connection. The director may also respond to the story by suggesting or eliciting a connection between a particular narrative and theological categories such as providence, salvation, call, community, forgiveness, grace, and so on. Finally, the director may respond by suggesting that the directee read or pray over a story from the tradition or contemporary community of faith that relates to the narrative.

Mary's retreat is again a case in point. Mary's psychological condition at the beginning of the retreat (when she is locked in her house and afraid to let anyone in) parallels the scene in the upper room on Easter night. When this was later mentioned to her during our interview, she responded very strongly to the suggestion: "I think probably, if I had had that passage, I would have realized that Jesus was already there and that would have been easier. I remember trying to open windows at home, and it was very hard for me to do that. So, yes, if I had had that image of Jesus having been in there, it would have been very helpful." Likewise, when asked during the interview which scripture most resembled her experience of "an exchange of love that took [her] beyond control...as if [she] were in a mystical garden," she immediately responded with the Song of Songs. Pointing her to that text or those themes in response to her description may have helped her stay in that loving embrace and perceive some precedent for her own experience in the tradition.

After reading storyteller and theologian John Shea's *An Experience Named Spirit*, Opal—the spiritual director-in-training mentioned above, who commented on her own need to tell and retell a particularly evocative experience—discovered the importance of her own Christian tradition in interpreting her story:

After reading [*An Experience Named Spirit*], I understood the necessity of having a referentially archetypal religious story in my life. It helped me understand the quality of what happened in my spiritually "coming back." Previously, I had personalized and privatized my religion and spirituality and had an amorphous Higher Power. This HP was still up there, out there, and intangible. It wasn't until I fused my historically, culturally recognized Jesus story with my secular story that I was able to see God's activity in my previous life (unconnected/unembodied) and current life (connected/embodied). I may occasionally resonate with certain Hindu or Buddhist stories/philosophies and they have been very helpful to me. However, because I am genetically and culturally "of the West" my religious story is bound in Christ.[55]

A spiritual director's ability to relate a directee's experience and story to the tradition may be one of the most crucial services he or she can render. A competent spiritual director acquires this ability through knowledge of the tradition and of his or her personal history. This conscious awareness of the tradition and personal experience, interpreted in the light of the tradition, supplies the director with both some tried-and true-categories for dealing with experiences, as well as the capacity to see things from multiple perspectives. Knowledge of the tradition opens this possibility, for, according to Gadamer, it has a rich and inherently contradictory character. The richness of the tradition and the conflicts within it do not generate a set of fixed categories but the ability to raise intelligent questions.

When a spiritual director can recognize in a directee's narrated experience something of the "variety of voices in which the echo of the past is heard,"[56] he or she can help the directee see it in the light of a whole host of stories or prior events. The ability to draw categories and frames of reference from the tradition relativizes the cultural concerns that, in part, constitute our contemporary "prejudices." These unconsciously determine the interpretive horizon in which the directee's experience is explored. One of the problems of the Catholic tradition, as transmitted through the late nineteenth century up to Vatican II, was the sense that the tradition carried a set of fixed answers instead of multiple ways of raising questions and responding to them with various alternatives.[57]

Subtle and seemingly indescribable experiences of God are historically conditioned even though they may appear to be timeless. The tradition shapes both a person's understanding of these experiences and provides a vocabulary for expressing them. A primary vocabulary comes from scripture, both its narratives and its poetry; the mystics supply yet another. Psychological language and practice, which tends to interpret experiences without reference to religious traditions, may provide a third vocabulary. If spiritual directors cannot connect their directees to their religious traditions, most of which predate contemporary psychology, they deprive them of the opportunity to experience a continuity of personal history with the larger tradition that is implicitly shaping their experience.

However a director responds, it is paramount that he or she profoundly respects the directee's sacred tale on its own terms. This response to actual stories occurs, first of all, by listening. Second, it ensures that discernment, elaboration, analysis, and interpretation are grounded in the concrete events, images, and details in the actual narrative in order to support the directee's self-understanding and perception of God's interaction with him or her in the context of the whole of life.

Questions for Further Reflection

1. As you reflect on your own story or those of your directees, can you identify "metaphors of the self" that organize your or their narrative identities? Do you have an image for each directee?

2. Have you noticed whether or not directees share with others as much of their private selves as they do with you? Do any directees have other people or groups with whom they can really share the religious dimension of their lives?

3. Can you give any examples of eliciting "the unsaid" in your directees' stories, either in the service of discernment or in helping directees notice more than they have been able to tell before?

4. As directees retell key stories, do you notice changes in each telling, or are directees merely repeating a "set" story?

5. How comfortable are you when directees begin to tell their "secrets," both difficult ones and sometimes their deepest religious experiences?

Chapter Five
We Tell a Story to Get a Story

The sacred tales that a directee tells in spiritual direction have several predictable and identifiable features. The primary theme is the directee's story of faith. A directee may tell this story explicitly and in great detail, or the story may simply be the implicit background for exploring many issues in the directee's life. Regardless of the storytelling in any given narrative session, the directee's story of faith provides the horizon for all other narrative activity. Quite literally, directees tell a story to get a story as they tell their sacred tales.

We have already characterized spiritual-direction narratives as an oral form of life story. Like all autobiographical accounts, directees create them in the present, in a serial fashion, and in a dialogical conversation with the director. This life story always remains unfinished, in medias res. Directors meet their directees for the first time in the middle of their directees' lives. There will always be many important prior events and experiences in their sacred stories that a director may never learn about. Directees selectively move from the present to key episodes in the past and back to the present in their stories. Because directees tell these stories usually in monthly sessions, their stories may introduce new characters or events in subsequent sessions without resolving unfinished plot lines from previous sessions. Finally, although spiritual-direction narratives have an affinity with other forms of life story—namely, biography, autobiography, and spiritual autobiography—the unique narrative situation makes spiritual-direction stories differ significantly from these other forms of life writing.

The Narrative Situation

The narrative situation of spiritual direction is ordinarily a face-to-face conversation between two people that takes place in an intimate and confidential setting. As chapter 2 described, both persons usually share the horizon of a common spiritual tradition and live within the larger story of Jesus and the community of his disciples. When spiritual direction is interdenominational or interfaith, these dynamics will differ significantly because their sacred horizons will not be the same. In addition, spiritual direction is a social influence process; the person seeking direction allows and even expects the director to be a shaping influence.[1] Because of the interactive nature of this process, the director serves as a conversation partner who responds to directees' narratives and often elicits further reflection and narration. These characteristics of the narrative situation of spiritual direction affect the telling of the story.[2]

According to counseling theory, a psychological process transpires between the two persons in a helping relationship. Spirituality professor Carolyn Gratton describes how the counselor "co-constitutes" the other: "It is after all, the counselor's unique personal perspective on reality, [his or] her relatively open or closed, broad or narrow, rigid or flexible perception of persons, events, and things that is the origin of [his or] her effective presence to the other."[3] The implicit understanding of what it means to be a human person proves important in this vision of reality. In the case of spiritual direction, the director must have a conscious awareness of his or her operative psychological theories of human experience and social process theories, as well as explicitly religious views that perceive the directee as loved by God and making some response to the grace offered.

This vision of another as constituted by God's concern

for that person is crucial to the spiritual-direction process and allows for quite diverse stories of God and the self. As noted in chapter 4, the human person's most significant identity is rooted in the God-human relationship. If this faith vision is true, then telling a story of God from the perspective of one's life experience may result in finding oneself in God. And conversely, telling a story of searching for the self may end in finding God in oneself. The director's vision of graced human reality would, in part, encourage directees to tell and retell their stories of searching for the self long enough to discover the transcendent dimension of all this searching.[4] This spiritual vision of the human person constitutes one of the primary differences between counseling or psychotherapy and spiritual direction. Spiritual direction also places persistent emphasis on conscious rather than unconscious experience. While therapy usually brackets the God question regardless of the specific beliefs of the therapist and the client, in spiritual direction both participants believe that God is the all-embracing context in which human life finds its meaning. This position assumes that God is understood in liberating and loving ways, as well as being utterly transcendent. Developmental psychologist Ronald Irwin, through his immersion in Buddhist practice, proposes a need to understand human flourishing beyond the confines of ego-generated identity narratives, however sophisticated the storying becomes. He suggests that this requires post-conventional psychological development, which results in an openness to meditative consciousness beyond ego control.

> If higher consciousness has a developmental dimension to it, then consciousness at higher stages may mean development that goes beyond early forms of ego control, development that goes beyond self-monitoring and self-surveillance, and the continual self-talk required for us to be conscientious citizens. Consciousness acquires a spaciousness, an openness, and a receptivity to inner realities and depths, without the operation of the ego's defenses

133

and conditionings. It is an openness to the entire sensorium free from the imposition of thought formations that always enforce an interpretation with reference to a center. It is a letting go, a surrendering, that leads to a nonattached acceptance of things as they are.[5]

Irwin further contrasts religion with spirituality, identifying religion with conformist levels of development, and spirituality with postconformist or postconventional forms of development.[6] While this is a tempting dichotomy to make, I think his distinctions might better be understood as the difference between exoteric, or formative dimensions of religion, and the esoteric, or mystical dimensions of major religious traditions. Within Christian tradition we call this mysticism or contemplation when we have such non-ego–generated experiences of the presence of God and the mystical consciousness that results from such encounters with transcendence.

The effect of a sacred horizon on storytelling in spiritual direction is quite powerful. With God as the horizon of all experience, the story makes explicit how life interacts with this mysterious horizon and interprets these experiences within a shared religious tradition. The spiritual-direction story constitutes a story of faith or a sacred tale, rather than a "story of Oedipal conflicts and their resolutions," as in a Freudian psychoanalytical conversation;[7] or the "story of individuation" in the Jungian framework; or the "story of development," as told from an Eriksonian perspective. The main plot is the story of faith, although other interpretive paradigms and stories of human experience may appear as subplots. In the case of Sam—the seminarian who was discerning ordination—his experience of psychoanalysis became one of the subplots in his spiritual-direction narrative. He tended to view his story of therapy as one of the ways God freed him to be more whole. He consciously experienced the healing brought about through the therapeutic process as grace. Despite his intense emotional pain, he felt God sustaining and accompanying him. His attraction to Jesus in his

agony in the garden concretely manifested this graced interpretation of his therapeutic story. In another narrative situation, such as therapy, a story of faith may appear as a subplot
but rarely is allowed to be the primary story.[8]

The climate created by the director's faith perspective and
an expansive hospitality encourages the directee's attempts to
articulate his or her spiritual identity and unique religious
experience. In other words, psychologically, the spiritual perspective of the director becomes a factor in "co-constituting"
the religious dimension of the person seeking direction. The
fact that both director and directee explicitly share a common
faith horizon or at least a faith horizon makes this the context
of all the narrative activity taking place within it.

The Life Story

The story told in direction is an oral version of spiritual
autobiography; directees gradually construct their spiritual
identity narratives when they tell a story of God in and through
their own life stories. Writer Jill Ker Conway emphasizes that it
"matters how we remember things." The way we remember
determines the plot that guides our future. She says:

> If we remember the past as a series of chaotic events
> governed by an impersonal and nonmoral fate or
> luck, we create a similar kind of future in our mind's
> eyes, and that prophecy is usually self-fulfilling. If
> we see the past as fully determined—by economic
> forces, by genetic codes, even by birth order and
> relationships with parents—we see ourselves as vic-
> tims of those forces, with our best hope a kind of
> stoic resignation. If we see our past as a moral spir-
> itual journey in time, our imagined future will con-
> tinue that quest.[9]

As in formal autobiography, the directee tells his or her
own story in the first person and is both the narrator and the

subject. In chapter 4, we saw in Dan McAdams' postmodernist work that "I" is telling the story of "me." And Scholes and Kellogg say that the lapse of time between experiencing the events and narrating them provides enough distance to "allow for all the potentially ironical divergence in point of view between character and narrator that a novelist could require."[10] Thus, the directee features himself or herself as the major character, the hero or heroine, in the story. As the storyteller, the directee already gains some distance from the events and begins to gain some objectivity in the telling.

Spiritual-direction conversations facilitate a continual process of reinterpretation of the directee's past experience from the perspective of the present. Like all autobiography, the story is told in the present. The current meaning and pattern the directee gives to his or her life encompasses the person's life prior to this spiritual-direction relationship. Significant "new experience," according to Gadamer, confounds expectations. Thus "new experience" provides a new perspective that directees then integrate into their self-presentation. As English professor Barrett J. Mandel says: "Autobiography forges present meaning into the marrow of one's remembered life."[11]

In spiritual direction, the directee tells a tale that includes this present sense of his or her life and its meaning; however, unlike a formal autobiography the narrator does not necessarily tell his or her life story from the vantage point of some important public achievement. Rather, directees fashion their life stories from the ordinary events of present experience.

For the director, beginning a series of spiritual-direction conversations embodies the narrative convention of in medias res. Many details presented early in a literary autobiography, especially episodes and significant material from the distant past, tend to emerge only in the form of "flashbacks," when an incident in the present evokes a specific memory from the past. The near past and the present experience of the person form the usual temporal focus, and the directee narrates events from the more distant past only when they provide information that the director seems to need or that directly relates to the present experience.

Sam's case demonstrates this temporal feature, although he left out his accounts of past experience from his written story. He restricted his initial self-presentation to major issues in spiritual direction and the events occurring during the prior academic year. He only referred to the more distant past when he described himself as an adult child of an alcoholic father. Not until later, when Sam wanted his director to understand his experience in therapy, would he occasionally tell a story about a paradigmatic episode from childhood that illustrated his point. For instance, he portrayed his father's characteristic manner of relating to him by describing how his father reacted when he graduated from high school. Mary's case makes this even clearer. Her recently failed marriage challenged her sense of herself and clearly impacted the present moment of her retreat experience. Her director then gently reminded her about episodes she had previously related to him in order to help make some connection between her earlier story and her present one.

Spiritual-direction narratives require a level of self-disclosure that surpasses the restraints of formal autobiography. As the history of spiritual direction surveyed in the introduction makes clear, spiritual direction requires the disclosure of the directee's motivation, temptations, confusions, and ambiguities, as well as painful and pleasant psychological and spiritual experiences. During eras when spiritual direction occurred in the context of the sacrament of confession, the directee's self-disclosure included actual sinful behavior, which public autobiography normally excluded.[12] Many details that most of us restrict to the private self are currently expressed with abandon on talk shows and in various Internet venues without much regard for the public nature of such disclosure in U.S. culture. Asian directees, however, are very reticent to reveal personal details of their lives even in spiritual direction. For North American directees, spiritual direction provides a much safer place to explore the ambiguous dimensions of many experiences.

This level of self-disclosure is possible because the director plays the role of a trusted intimate. This sense of privacy and, even more important, a trust in the confidentiality of the narrative situation support the directee's tentative efforts to express himself or herself non-defensively. In a fruitful relationship, the directee presumes that the director is a friendly ally whom the directee does not ordinarily need to persuade to respond favorably. This attitude contrasts sharply with the strong rhetorical emphasis in memoirs or apologia, which relate a life story specifically to defend the author against a public attack or an alternative perception of events.

The directee's self-knowledge and insight about his or her own situation constitutes one of the purposes of this storytelling. This insight is a result of the directee's freedom to discover his or her desires, motives, and actions through the stories told to the director. The privacy and spontaneity of the narrative situation in spiritual direction tend to produce life stories that are less self-consciously organized around preselected patterns than formal autobiographies are. As more highly patterned stories, formal autobiographies omit experiences or events that do not clearly fit the design. By contrast, spiritual-direction narratives tend to include such experiences because they have not yet been fully assimilated into the life story.

Pattern and Selectivity

As the stories of spiritual direction demonstrate, a spiritual-direction narrative begins with the first direction session. This first interview is usually tentative and exploratory. Ordinarily, the directee begins by telling the director about his or her life, during which the directee attempts to test out if he or she feels sufficiently comfortable with this person to continue and whether or not the director will be helpful. The director usually helps the directee disclose enough of his or her background and current situation for the director to get a sense whether he or she can work with this person. Because of the exploratory nature of this conversation, directees vary considerably in the depth of self-disclosure they will risk in initial meetings, especially since some will interview two or three directors before committing to the relationship.

Sam's initial interview represents a high level of self-disclosure and a willingness to take risks. He revealed a great deal in the first session and made himself very vulnerable. Sam already knew his spiritual director socially as a classmate, so he could presume she knew his more general background, as well as the local context that they shared. Because he disclosed several emotionally charged and important recent experiences in this first session, she waited for him to fill in the details of family and community history as their conversations continued over the year. This occurred gradually, characteristically in the "flashback" mode when he needed to interpret present experience in the light of his past history. On the other hand, Mary was hesitant and guarded in sharing her story. She found it very difficult to articulate what was happening to her, and her process of disclosure took several retreats. Understandably, her director was cautious about inviting elaboration, based on her earlier reluctance.

Although some writers on spiritual direction advise that directors need a thorough account of a person's history, in practice this seems to take place when the directee feels secure enough to share this story from the past.[13] Directors usually find it appropriate for directees to talk about anything that seems relevant to their life of faith and experience of God, as it is interwoven with life experience. Unlike a therapeutic situation, contemporary spiritual direction is not necessarily "problem oriented," and, in contrast to the post-Tridentine model, the required story no longer begins with "sin."

Because of its oral mode and particular context, the spiritual-direction narrative includes only selected details. Determining which details to include often depends on the directee's perception of the director and his or her understanding of spiritual direction, as well as his or her present challenges and emotional situation. Because directees shape their stories for a particular director, they choose details that establish common ground between them. The director affects the directee's narrative by the quality of attention given to particular topics or issues. The director may demonstrate interest by his or her quality of presence, by questions offered to the directee, or by other interpretive comments. Directees tend to omit topics that seem to bore the director or to which the director makes no response.

In addition to the actual responses of a director, literary critical theory suggests that the director receives the projections of the "implied audience" or "implied reader" created by the narrator.[14] The storyteller projects an image of what a spiritual director is interested in and shapes the narrative accordingly. Sam probably based the first half of his opening narrative on such a projection, for he knew his director in a very limited way. The director is asked to play a variety of roles by this fictive projection and, as indicated by his or her responses, can choose to respond according to the way the narrative marks out the role, choose to refuse the projection, or choose to accept or reject some part of it.[15]

Once a direction relationship has been initiated, the pattern of narration unfolds within the structure of a serial and results in an episodic structure. Each session constitutes its own discrete narrative unit; the narrative units following the initial interview usually consist of separate episodes that have occurred since the last meeting. The time between sessions, like starting a new chapter in a novel, allows the storyteller to introduce new characters or leave a plot line unfinished temporarily.[16] In the spiritual-direction conversation, the intervening time and the purpose of direction make considerable discontinuity in the narrative acceptable.

In creating their narratives, directees select events that seem most important from among those they have experienced. In a sense, though, *life* does the selecting.[17] The directee's initial selection of both subjects and sequences of action (plots) already forms "a kind of plot" that represents some "tension" point seeking resolution. The directee begins to fashion connections among the events through the narrative process. Directees frequently select the themes for their stories from among the following experiences: an unresolved conflict, a troublesome experience, a particular sense of God interacting with them during prayer or through some other event, the effects of social reality, the invitation to change or grow, their relationships, or something related to work or ministry. Typically, these events may be "high points" or "low points," although people in a relatively problem-free period may tell stories of simple, ordinary, and subtle experiences of grace that tend to go unnoticed during more turbulent times.

Each incident chosen for narration may at first seem distinct with no apparent connection to the other narrative units in the same conversation or during the previous session. Occasionally these incidents seem related only because they occurred within the same two- or three-week period of time. However, each incident is set off against all the preceding segments. Gradually, a story emerges because of the reciprocal relationships among the narrative elements.[18] Stylistically, one might describe these units as cinema verité excerpts.[19]

Gradually, both the directee and the director begin to create coherency and connections among the disparate stories. If Iser is correct, in this shared narrative activity, the director gets as involved as the storyteller in looking for connections among the stories. Unity of narration emerges in several ways. It inheres in the narrative voice, the "I" who provides a consistent narrative perspective in each episode, even though the protagonist of each episode may or may not be the directee. From this continuous narrative voice, the directee's character gradually reveals itself to the director. The unity of narration also emerges, gradually, in motifs and themes (the values and meanings espoused)[20] that the narrator finds compelling. In addition, the unity of narration consists in a characteristic repetition of behaviors and attitudes on the part of the protagonist. This element matches a novelistic interest in a "developing character," which provides an incipient plot structure for the sequential narrative units.[21]

Discontinuities in the story, however, are also common. Characteristically, in each session there are many interwoven plots in the life story. A narrative sequence storied in one session may or may not be resumed in the next. The director/listener learns to avoid sheer curiosity—wondering, "What happened next?"—when a story breaks off at the end of a session and is not taken up in the next. The directee's life may have moved to a new center of interest or to another plot, leaving the listener with an incomplete story line. While refraining from forcing the story line into the trajectory indicated by the last session, the listener/director remains attentive to that theme when the narrator develops this particular plot line in a subsequent session. In some cases, the director may need to return to a theme or plot line, especially if she or he suspects that the broken-off plot line represents unresolved or suppressed issues, rather than merely an unfinished story of already completed action for the directee. The director needs to discriminate between an incomplete narrative and the directee's inability to assimilate some experiences into the narrated life.[22]

Some Differences between Men's and Women's Narratives

In addition to the narrative features described above, the narrative styles of men and women show significant differences. Feminist literary-critical studies of autobiography contrast a unidirectionality in men's lives with a multidimensionality in women's lives. Men's unidirectionality finds its narrative counterpart in a linear narrative in which men unify their stories by concentrating on one theme, period, or characteristic of their personalities. By contrast, women's lives, rooted in their flexible social roles, are more frequently characterized by a multidimensionality, which creates a pattern of diffusion and diversity: "The narratives of their lives are often not chronological and progressive, but disconnected, fragmentary, or organized into self-sustained units rather than connecting chapters."[23] Literary critic Suzanne Juhasz makes this point even more concrete:

142

> When you ask a woman, "What happened?" you often get an answer in the style that McClelland has labeled circumstantial, complex, and contextual.... The woman is omitting no detail that she can remember, because all details have to do with her sense of the nature of "what happened." A man, on the other hand, will characteristically summarize: give you the gist, the result, the point of the event. In their form, women's lives tend to be like the stories that they tell. They show less a pattern of linear development towards some clear goal[24] than one of repetitive, cumulative, cyclical structure.[25]

In spiritual direction, women tend to narrate their lives with a wealth of detail, affect, and imagery.[26] Directors operating from a masculine point of view have often seen this as negative, judging the wealth of detail as unnecessary or irrelevant. This perspective fails to appreciate that this narrative style corresponds to the way women experience their lives. Women characteristically attend to several types of experience simultaneously without necessarily unifying them in relationship to each other. Frequently, the opportunity to tell the story creates a unity of its own without achieving a unified plot in its first telling.[27]

Men exhibit contrasting characteristics in their storytelling. They tend to control their narrative self-disclosure by limiting affective and descriptive detail. Typically, men emphasize actions or meanings. One sentence in objective language can both conceal and reveal intense affective experiences. The male tendency toward unidirectionality in storytelling, while often refreshing, can be a drawback. Men may believe that they have told the whole story with great economy of expression and in a highly unified pattern, while they actually may have left out the story more appropriate to spiritual direction. For this reason, men frequently require an invitation to expand the description. Directors with male directees will elicit much that would remain "unsaid" if they did not listen for material beneath the surface of the story.

The facilitation of the director can help male directees explore and become comfortable with the emotional aspects of their experience and then incorporate this into their particular form of the male story without unnecessarily threatening their self-image.

Sam's case demonstrates some aspects of male affectivity as it emerged in his story. Although usually aware of his feelings, Sam did not feel altogether comfortable disclosing them. He, nevertheless, reported his feelings of embarrassment during the session in which he agreed to visualize a feeling he could not yet name. In a second instance when he described his experience at the diaconal ordination as "having lost it," he showed how men typically first present emotionally positive experiences in a negative form. The negative judgment about loss of self-control reflected his male conditioning: men are not supposed to cry in public, even in a liturgy. His first telling of this story reinforced this conditioning. When pressed to be more concrete about what happened before "losing it," Sam described an interior, felt sense of being called to ordination and of being lovable and acceptable to God *just as he was*. The invitation to tell more of his story allowed him to tell this much more important story as the main plot, instead of the embarrassment over losing emotional control. The story of love and acceptance became the primary plot, rather than the story of crying in public. Retelling the story in this way matched the more important affect with narrative form, allowing the depth of the experience to remain present in memory as well as in its emotional effect. By telling this story differently, the masculine narrator can resist the pressure of dominant, male, social norms, at least within the privacy of spiritual direction.

The director's responses to the narratives told by men and by women need to take into account their differences. With a woman directee, the director can very helpfully extrapolate two or three major themes from a great quantity of narrational detail. Naming them for her may be revelatory and helpful, as she may not yet have become explicitly conscious of them as themes. Focusing on one episode and exploring it in depth can allow her to see the entire story in a new light. With men, directors often face the challenge of eliciting greater detail and nuance, especially with regard to feelings. The male directee, who is more likely to censor aspects of the story that feel too chaotic or confusing, needs reassurance that he can talk about an experience that he has not already fully understood.

Telling Stories of the Experience of God

Many people seeking spiritual direction find that their central task consists of learning to tell how they experience God and live their life story within the larger story of Christian faith. Experiences of God remain among the most difficult to articulate. U.S. culture has made it easier for some people to describe and tell stories of peak experiences since the 1960s, but only so long as their interpretations are secular and the experiences themselves are triggered by drugs, sex, or music. Beginning in the 1980s, a privatized version of the born-again Christian fundamentalist story became a permitted and encouraged religious narrative within those communities. As mentioned in chapter 2, this religious story is often antimodernist. Stories, however, about a strangely loving Mystery—that subtly allures one and insists on a response—remain difficult to tell, even in the spiritual-direction situation. There are no established cultural forms for these highly personal and unique encounters with the Holy, for these experiences of being flooded with love and care, gentleness and acceptance, call and challenge. Habits of language and social convention work against telling one another our deepest stories of life and meaning, especially if suffused with strong feelings. It seems that the story in our culture that initially requires being "told slant," to use an image from Emily Dickenson,[28] is the story that emerges from religious depths. These deep stories of the self and God, stories of mystical experience and self-transcendence, are among the "secrets" directees learn to tell in spiritual direction, secrets that are not necessarily welcome even in religious circles.

Through these kinds of experience, one becomes aware of that which eludes comprehension and utterly transcends the human person. We call that which transcends us "Mystery," or, in theologian Karl Rahner's phrase, "Holy Mystery."[29] We do not, however, always experience this mystery as elusive or something just beyond our reach; sometimes we experience it as a transcendence that comes toward us, breaking in on our everyday existence in a mysterious way as gift. Theologian Denis Edwards names this type of religious event an "experience of grace."[30]

Spiritual direction helps people identify and talk about such moments. It provides an opportunity for them to explore and tell the sacred tales of their own relationship with this holy Mystery; it also frees them from inadequate or inaccurate images of God or from the burden of "ought's" and "should's" about what a relationship with God entails. People often have difficulty recognizing a similarity between their "churchy," conventional expectations of God and these more general, less conventionally "religious" experiences of God as the ground and horizon of their being.

Such experiences of God are characterized by an atmosphere of mystery, understood as a strange presence that intrudes into a person's life. The mood of the narration is often reverent and filled with awe, and includes a mixture of both attraction and fear. The listener responds with a corresponding awe in receiving this story. Although fear of this strangely uncontrolled and uncontrollable reality may be present, there often exists a more-fundamental tone of joy and gratitude—a conviction that the reality present in this mode has significance and meaning for the directee. Stories such as these draw on the ecological and relational selves described by Ulric Neisser in chapter 4 because these experiences are sensed, felt, but are not easy to incorporate into the autobiographical self. They also tend to feel intensely private.

Only after honoring these experiences of mystery and

telling them interiorly or in the context of spiritual direction do people grasp with any degree of coherence how God interacts with them in and through their personality, history, relationships, level of psychological development, and activities. Learning to tell this story of grace enables the directee to grow in responsiveness to this experience. In traditional language, we would consider this responsiveness as growth in faith, hope, and love. The person's life becomes increasingly oriented toward God in all of its dimensions. The unique pattern and specific interactions with God, who both encompasses the whole of the person's life and remains always beyond grasp, rise to the directee's conscious awareness and demand a response.

Theologian and author John Shea points out how contemporary culture makes it very difficult to receive these experiences of mystery. The technological spirit of the age fosters a manipulative, controlling, restricting attitude toward the environment and other people, rather than a receptive, contemplative, or appreciative one: "Although the technological spirit does not mean automatic insensitivity to mystery, we do live in an age tempted to a secular restriction on consciousness. This temptation is often caricatured as the flat-earth impulse, the tendency to level all vertical awareness to a horizontal understanding. Anything that smacks of transcendence is immediately flattened."[31]

Because the culture does not foster an awareness of mystery, many people need help identifying these experiences. We need to hear stories about encountering mystery that might serve as contemporary narrative models, and we especially need stories that take place in everyday life, not in religious settings or described by a religious vocabulary.[32] Frequently, notions about the experience of God prove too narrow to include encounters that take place outside of prayer. An example may illustrate these difficulties more clearly:

A farmer who had agreed, reluctantly, to attend a workshop on Christian faith found himself confronted with the question: "Is there any special time in your life when you find yourself overwhelmed by a sense that there is something more than yourself involved, something more than you can account for, a time when something seems like a gift given from beyond yourself?" For the first time, in a session lasting several hours, the farmer's face showed interest, and after a while he volunteered a comment: "I feel like that sometimes in the early mornings when I am out in the middle of a crop of wheat and I hold a grain of new wheat in my hand." He went on to say that he had never talked to anyone about this experience before, even though it had happened over many years. The experience had been so overwhelming as to be almost inexpressible, and he had felt that others would not understand what he was talking about. As the discussion continued it became clear that, while the farmer went to church regularly, and sometimes prayed, he had never, to this point, explicitly connected his experience in his wheat crop with anything in his Christian faith.[33]

Both John Shea and Denis Edwards specify a number of occasions or "triggers" that may initiate just such experiences of mystery—if a person grasps this dimension of them. Edwards uses the broad categories of experiences of "richness and abundance" and those of "limit or vulnerability." Experiences of richness and abundance, which surpass what can be attributed to the human participants alone, include interpersonal love, creativity, forgiveness, childbirth, parenting, and beauty. Among the experiences of limit or vulnerability are death, failure, loneliness, and alienation. These limit-experiences often disclose a depth dimension or a loving presence that comes to one in, and through, a painful or frightening situation. In each experience of limit, the situation evokes or changes into a qualitatively different experience, which becomes the experience of mystery. Ellen's spiritual direction with Karla in chapter 4 shows this subtle movement. In her feelings of human loneliness, Ellen had not noticed that she was also accompanied by God and could say, "He had to be there."[34]

In *Stories of Faith*, John Shea talks about revelatory encounters with mystery as an ordinary and unavoidable human process. He finds in these experiences five elements that one can analyze, even though the people involved may never articulate these elements to themselves. Shea describes these elements as follows:

1. There is a relationship to the mystery of life.
2. This mystery communicates meanings about the nature of the relationship.
3. This meaning is initially formulated and then pondered, acted on, rephrased, repondered, reacted on, and so on.
4. The meaning that is received is related to the conflicts, questions, and needs of the people involved.
5. Although there is an enshrined religious vocabulary to talk about the felt perception of these experiences, it is seldom used. This last element is a special characteristic of contemporary revelation-faith experiences.[35]

Shea aptly describes some narrative features of these encounters with mystery and how people appropriate the meanings disclosed in the experiences. First of all, each experience Shea describes finds its way into a storytelling situation. A salesman tries to tell another about something that "struck" him when out with a friend they both knew. In another, a college girl tells her family how she felt upon hearing Mother Teresa speak. In a third, a man in his mid-forties tells the rest of his family what he spontaneously said to his dying father. In each instance, the person who has encountered the mystery dimension of life struggles to articulate something about the experience to another person.

As noted in chapter 4, people often tell such stories several times so that they can adequately grasp and formulate the meaning of an experience. Once they can articulate the value or truth through these multiple tellings, a meaning emerges that may become a touchstone for the future. The kind of truth found in these "faith formulations," however, may seem quite arbitrary if separated from the unique events that generated it; we need to keep in mind the provisional kind of truth that arises in a life story.[36] Every such meaning is liable to revision on the basis of a new experience of relationship with Mystery.

Shea's fourth element treats the relationship between the meaning developed from the encounter with Mystery and the person's particular preoccupations. These might include questions, crises, and life situation at the time. Thus, the college girl interprets her response to Mystery in terms of commitment and the ideals that govern her life choices. The salesman, not far from retirement, interprets his experience in terms of relationships with grandchildren. The man whose father died talks about "letting go," an appropriate response to the surrender death requires. In Sam's case, he interprets his experience at the diaconal ordination and to the song "I Need You" in relationship to his vocational discernment. Mary's identification with the paschal Mystery clearly relates to the pain of her divorce and its aftermath.

Finally, Shea's last point about the language chosen to articulate these experiences offers an important linguistic clue to the secular vocabulary many contemporary people adopt for religious experience. He argues that, even in a culture that does not adequately provide a specific vocabulary for these experiences, nonetheless, they are neither lost nor left unexpressed. Rather, they are expressed in a "more subtle use of secular language," and he gives the following examples: "That's what it's all about;" "Without this it wouldn't be worth living;" "That's damnable;" "A life without love is tragic;" "It's pathetic the way she is squandering her youth."[37] These expressions hint at a larger dimension in life.

Shea also points out how people often speak, not of the things of life, but about "life" itself. He considers this a linguistic clue indicating that the underlying experience has been revelatory and interpreted in a faith mode.[38]

Several directors identified other linguistic clues that signal narratives of experiences with Mystery in their practice of spiritual direction. When directees begin to tell these stories, some change occurs. "Either the story stops for a while, and the directee lapses into silence, or speech becomes more halting as people search for language."[39] Describing authentic religious experience usually requires reliance on metaphorical expression, as described in chapter 3, which often has a fresh and unique character to it.

In the contemporary model of spiritual direction, the directee is encouraged to tell a sacred tale of unique religious experience usually noticed as interior movements, subtle changes in oneself that suggest God is at work, or the experiences of revelation that Shea describes. When these experiences happen in the midst of complex life-events rather than during times of solitude or prayer, they often go unnoticed and unarticulated unless the recipient engages in the telling and retelling that happens in spiritual direction and in some other faith-sharing groups.[40] God is also often found in church and in explicitly religious practices. This chapter has emphasized experience of God that happens within the context of ordinary life, into which God inserts God's self in some noticeable but unexpected way. These experiences are more difficult to sense and to talk about. Many people continue to participate in liturgy and in a round of personal prayer and devotional practices, because they experience a change in themselves when they do. These stories, too, benefit from being told as a sacred tale in spiritual direction because the meanings and sense of relationship are unique for each person.

Questions for Further Reflection

1. As a spiritual director, how do you make a decision about whether to bring up something from an unfinished story

that began in a previous session or to wait for the directee to return to that plot?

2. How does thinking about spiritual direction as a serial story with multiple plot lines help you as a director make connections between sessions and among the stories?

3. What kinds of language and speech patterns are clues for you that a directee is beginning to talk about a story of faith?

4. What stories are easiest to tell in spiritual direction and which are the most difficult?

5. How does God's presence make itself felt in the directee's story and in the spiritual-direction session?

6. Do your directees have any narrative opportunities other than spiritual direction to tell their stories of Mystery?

Conclusion
Unpredictable Interventions, Annunciations, and Invitations

One of the greatest surprises for beginning spiritual directors is how much their directees' stories and struggles affect *them* as spiritual directors from session to session. Novelist Amy Tan describes the effect of a good story on her:

> It can enlarge us by helping us notice small details in life. It can remind us to distrust absolute truths, to dismiss clichés, to both desire and fear stillness, to see the world freshly from closer up or farther away, with a sense of mystery or acceptance, discontent or hope, all the while remembering that there are so many possibilities, and that this was only one.
>
> The best stories do change us. They help us live interesting lives.[1]

As a fiction writer, Tan describes the creative possibilities of having many different story lines, moods, visions of life, characters, and experiences of God. It is always possible to change the story. When we take a narrative approach to spiritual direction, we immerse ourselves as directors in a world of stories not our own, but that converge with ours and influence them. We have seen in previous chapters that the religious dimension of these stories is continually present. When we remember that these stories of grace, of revelation, of mystery, of conversion, of call, of commitment, of discipleship—of ministry and service, love and devotion, work and family life—transpire in a God-soaked atmosphere, we approach them as sacred tales, openings through story into how God enters our lives and changes them. We become ever more susceptible to the unpredictable interventions, annunciations, and invitations of God's Spirit in our world. These stories are created not only between the director and directee in the sacred narrative opportunity of spiritual direction; they are also co-created by God's Spirit within the spiritual-direction setting, influencing both director and directee, as well as revealing God's mysterious activities in the directee's daily life. For both directors and directees, every moment is potentially open to an unexpected intervention, annunciation, or invitation.

The Effects of Directees' Sacred Tales on the Director

The director, as we have seen, actively participates in the directee's storytelling during the process of spiritual direction. Because stories draw in their listeners emotionally, intellectually, and imaginatively, the director finds himself or herself living within the directee's story. If the director genuinely participates as a partner in search of the fuller meaning of the directee's story, the truth that emerges from this cooperative dialogue—the truth in images, feelings, sensations, and thoughts—directly addresses him or her. According to Hans-Georg Gadamer, that truth is valid for both people.[2] The emergence of a truth that belongs to both persons results from the mutuality and reciprocity in all "I-Thou" relationships. There is always a form of communion and mutuality between two people in an authentic relationship. As Gadamer states: "The experience of the 'Thou' must be a specific one, in that the 'Thou' is not an object but is in relationship with us."[3]

Gadamer contrasts this kind of experience of the "Thou" with one that

> seeks to discover things that are typical in the
> behavior of one's fellow men [and women] and is
> able to make predictions concerning another per-
> son on the basis of experience. We call this knowl-
> edge of human nature. We understand the other
> person in the same way that we understand any
> other typical event in our experiential field, i.e., he
> [or she] is predictable.[4]

This approach denies the dynamic mutuality in the relationship that is open to something entirely new. Seeking pre-
dictability results in turning the other into some "typical"
category, eliminating the possibility of mutual influence and
the possibility of personally being profoundly addressed and
affected by what the other says.

Gadamer describes a third type of experience of the
"Thou," in which one person controls the conversation by
imposing his or her interpretation on the experience of the
other. In this mode, the "Thou" is acknowledged, but, despite
trying to understand the other, the person is relating more to
himself or herself than to the other.

> This relation is not immediate, but reflective. To
> every claim there is a counter-claim. That is why it
> is possible for each of the partners in the relation-
> ship reflectively to outdo the other. One claims to
> express the other's claim and even to understand
> the other better than he [or she] understands him-
> self [or herself]. In this way the "Thou" loses the
> immediacy with which it makes its claim. It is
> understood, but this means that it is anticipated
> and interpreted reflectively from the standpoint of
> the other person.[5]

The attempt of one partner in the conversation to remove
him- or herself from the other's influence is harmful to the
spiritual-direction relationship. In spiritual direction, the
director wants to facilitate the directee's growth in his or her

core spiritual identity as he or she encounters God. Nothing fruitful for the directee can occur if the director alters the direction of the relationship in an effort to dominate the other or resist the claims of the other person's life on him or her.[6]

The director receives the gift of the directee's story in this mutual process and also risks being challenged and changed by this unique story of grace. The director receives, first of all, by participating in the directee's meaning-making process. The revelatory truth about life and relationship to the Holy that emerges from the directee's religious experience enhances or challenges the director's own process of meaning making. If the meaning that emerged mutually and collaboratively in the spiritual-direction conversation is compelling and valid, then it exerts an influence and can make a claim on the director's life as well as on the directee's. Directees become characters in the director's life story, just as directors become characters in the stories of their directees; for example, Sam, Mary, and Ellen described how important their directors became for them. A directee's willingness to disclose his or her spiritual identity and to talk about how Ultimate Reality has addressed and transformed his or her life encourages and challenges the director to live in relationship to the same ultimate Mystery that the directee experiences. Sam's experience of being unconditionally loved "just as he was" profoundly affected his director: if God loved Sam in this way and called him to ordination, didn't God love his director in the very same way? Sam's response to his call to priesthood and religious life invited his director to a renewed fidelity to her own religious commitments. Although directors do not ordinarily discuss their responses with the directee, they are often, nonetheless, affected. They then can allow the directee's story to address them or they can resist its impact.

Because the directee and director usually share some version of the same faith tradition, the directee's faith story can become a contemporary proclamation of the "gospel" to the director. At the very least, in interfaith spiritual direction, both believe in and relate to God from within their particular traditions. In spiritual direction, the relationship between director and directee differs markedly from a therapeutic situation, which does not presume the therapist and client share similar values and beliefs. In spiritual direction, both the director and the directee are addressed by, and stand within, a common or similar faith tradition. Insofar as the directee's life story genuinely embodies a concrete aspect of that faith tradition, it addresses the director and challenges him or her to respond to God's influence beyond his or her role as a spiritual director.

Without a capacity for genuine openness to the directee and to the unpredictable interventions, annunciations, and invitations of God's Spirit, the director will remain unaffected by his or her life story:

> In human relations the important thing is, as we have seen, to experience the "Thou" truly as a "Thou," i.e., not to overlook his [or her] claim and to listen to what he [or she] has to say to us. To this end, openness is necessary. But this openness exists ultimately not only for the person to whom one listens, but rather anyone who listens remains fundamentally open. Without this kind of openness to one another there is no genuine human relationship. Belonging together always also means being able to listen to one another. When two people understand each other, this does not mean that one person "understands" the other, in the sense of surveying him....Openness to the other, then, includes the acknowledgement that I must accept some things that are against myself, even though there is no one else who asks this of me.[7]

When this type of relationship exists in spiritual direction, the director finds that he or she constantly learns from the directee. By welcoming the authenticity of the directee's unique experience, the director gradually grows in his or her capacity to exercise *phronesis,* as discussed in chapter 2. Indeed, directors expand their life experience through their directees' sacred tales. Hearing many stories about how good people actually resolve and respond to a variety of challenges and life situations enlarges the range of possible actions for directors in their own lives and for the directees they influence. Directors not only find new ways to respond in a particular situation, they also modify and adapt their ideal of a "good person" (character in the moral sense) on the basis of how good people actually behave.

Directors often think of their spiritual-direction sessions in terms of a "sacramental" experience. Theologian and storyteller John Shea defines *sacramental* in this context as experiencing God acting in and through an ordinary human experience. In and through these rich conversations with directees, the director experiences God acting and alive in the world. God is acting and alive in the directees' lives in between sessions, as well as in the sessions themselves.

Sharing faith experience through these sacred tales frequently becomes moments of communion, and thus a directee's story may affect the director. In telling stories of faith, directees relive their own experiences and witness to them. At the same time, the director imaginatively participates in the directee's story through his or her interest, openness, and deep listening for grace, frequently experienced in and through the directee. God actively intervenes and becomes present within the spiritual-direction setting. Jesuit liturgist Paul Janowiak described this kind of experience when he talked about how one directee affected him:

> Just yesterday, after I had finished with someone, I recognized that I was harried from the week when I began the direction session. During the session, this woman directee had been describing her feeling of being deeply graced during the week. She had been talking about Mary and waiting for Jesus to be born. When I was setting up the next appointment, I said to her: "I just want to tell you that every time

you come and we have these sharings, I always end
up feeling more whole."[8]

Paul's directee changed his emotional state from feeling "har-
ried" to "feeling more whole." Sharing his directee's contemplative experience of "waiting for Jesus to be born" had the
effect of restoring him to a more centered place in himself.
Apparently, this was a consistent experience for him with
this directee. In turn, he chose to share with her the effect
she had on him and, by doing so, reflected back to her the
quality of her own consciousness.

A second way the directee's story may affect the director
is by stimulating the director's memories of his or her own
religious history. For example, as Sam understood how God's
activity and his own responses indicated the appropriateness
of his decision, his director may have relived her equally
unique experiences that led to her perpetual profession as a
religious sister. His story of grace evoked both the similarities and the differences in her story. To a certain extent, both
director and directee shared the same story because they
both shared a religious tradition that has historically maintained a particular, institutional style of religious living.
However, the way they lived that story differed because of
gender and other personal differences. This shared tradition
served as the horizon within which they both interpreted
their experiences of call and response.

A third way directors may be affected is through disagreements with their directees' interpretation of events. For
example, a directee may present the distilled meaning of an
experience as, "All real life is meeting." The director may not
immediately agree with this conclusion. To resolve this type
of dissonance, the director frequently elicits more of the
directee's story, tracing the evolution of this "truth" from the
concrete situation and from the questions or conflicts con-
fronting the directee at that moment. When the directee's formulation is put in the fuller context of how it emerged,
cognitive disagreements may dissolve.

Frequently, however, such an evolution of truth may not

apply to the director at all because his or her life situation differs from the directee's. According to John Shea, "What happens in the revelation-faith experience is closely connected to what is happening in us before the experience. The needs that are troubling us, the drives that are urging us on, the conflicts we are engaged in shape the content of the revelation."[9] Thus, the meaning that a directee derives from a given experience may be limited, perhaps applicable to a single specific experience. Such a meaning may also be rooted in an operational or denominational theology that differs remarkably with the director's.

Sometimes these differences in the interpretation of events may not be able to be resolved at the session and will require help from supervision or consultation. At other times, however, once the formula is traced back through the directee's story, the more fully elaborated story may suggest a broader range of possible meanings that address both the directee's and the director's lives.

This possible surplus of meanings is rooted in the nature of narrative and the meaning-making activities of the director/listener. Narratives do not present a single possible meaning or truth. Rather, the complexity of perspectives provided by the plot, characters, narrator, and implied reader invites the listener/reader to create his or her meaning for the narrative as it unfolds. Different directors may arrive at different, yet equally valid meanings from the narrative clues. Thus, directors actively engage in the process of meaning making from the interplay of these perspectives as they follow the story being told.

According to literary critic Wolfgang Iser, the reader/listener actively projects possible scenarios in relationship to the "blanks" in the story.[10] All of us naturally "fill in the blanks" as a story unfolds that leaves gaps of missing action and resolution. The serial nature of spiritual-direction stories tends to stimulate the director to make connections between parts of the story that the storyteller may not have necessarily made while telling it. Directors need to be aware that the connections between themes, actions, and meanings that the directee makes or, perhaps, does not even notice, may be very different from their own. Thus the director's creative engagement with the directee's unfolding story requires a certain amount of restraint and a testing out of potential connections with the directee. This conversation can be very rich for both the directee and the director and may lead to fresh illumination for both, but the director needs to be careful not to impose his or her meanings or connections on the directee's story. Some directors are such avid story followers they may not realize that the directee has not made the same connections.

A fourth way directors can be affected by their directees is by becoming part of their directees' stories. Spiritual directors may not be prepared to become an important character in their directees' stories. As developed earlier in this book, a relational understanding of the self suggests that, when we tell our own stories, we are also telling stories about the most significant people in our lives. If, indeed, we are selves-in-relation, we experience ourselves in relationship to parents and siblings, partners and lovers, classmates and teachers, bosses and coworkers, and a host of other people. Many of my former students who agreed to share their stories of spiritual direction gave me permission only after asking the permission of their spiritual directors even though their directors would never be identified. The students immediately recognized that when they told their own story, they were also telling a story about their directors.

Within the literary community that studies life writing, the ethics of telling someone else's story while telling one's own is producing a growing body of literature.[11] How accurate are the directees' characterization of us as directors, or, for that matter, their characterizations of other people in their lives? It is important for directors to remember they are hearing only one version of the story of a relationship. Having access to the other half of the story might change the director's perception of the other person. Just as directees become characters in the life story of the director, so too directors become characters in the directee's story. As Roy

Schafer says, "We narrate others as we narrate selves."[12] It can come as quite a surprise to discover that directors have no control over the way directees "narrate us" in the stories they tell others. Because directors and directees share different perspectives on their relationship and on the case history of a given spiritual-direction relationship, the story of a relationship is likely to both converge and differ from one another. While the director is obliged to maintain confidentiality about the directee, directees do not always maintain confidentiality about themselves or their directors. Frequently, the directee's account is very positive. At other times, it is not. And a director can do nothing to contest the directee's version of their experience.

Ellen described how Karla became part of her prayer experience as she contemplated Jesus on the beach with John and Peter. "I thought of Karla as a beloved disciple, recognizing Jesus when I do not and sometimes pointing him out, but mostly watching attentively until Jesus finds me." Here we see how Ellen's religious experience is supported by her relationship with Karla. In another session, Ellen wrote:

> Sometime in the early months of spiritual direction, I dipped into my not uncommon state of global distress: lethal poverty in New York, our devastation of Iraq, genocide in Darfur, and other horrors were dominating my consciousness. I figured that my state of mind would be a good topic of conversation with Karla. My basic question was: "How can I discern between what should concern me and what will merely paralyze me?" To my surprise, Karla said only eight words: "Whatever is important to God is never lost." That was it. I remember her words verbatim, and if I remember her demeanor correctly, she had no interest in discussing with me the death and destruction that was permeating the planet at that time. Her brief declaration made with certitude stunned me and preempted my discernment question.

I do not remember what followed during that session, but when I left her office, I noticed that my feeling of paralysis had dissipated. I was also aware that I had entered the office intent upon delving into my distress, but neither God nor Karla was willing to go along with my agenda. Many, many times since that day, when I have felt overwhelmed by people suffering or by destruction of God's creations, I have thought of Karla's eight words and tried to approximate her conviction. I have occasionally shared her statement with friends in distress, and the words seem to affect them in much the same way they affect me.

In this last example from Ellen, we glimpse another portrayal of Karla. In this session, Karla responds like a desert *amma* described in the introduction. To Ellen's preoccupation and distress, Karla responds with a "word," which functions very much like the sacramental "word" in the desert tradition, or like a Zen koan. In Ellen's case, these eight words shifted Ellen's focus and changed her energy. They challenged her to find a less destructive way to be with the world's suffering. These eight words became so important to Ellen that she shared them with others.

One final example from Ellen's story of spiritual direction with Karla demonstrates the way gospel stories acquire fresh meaning when encountered in relationship to a particular life situation. Ellen wrote:

One rare Sunday morning when I was not especially pressed for time, I contemplated the passage in Matthew about the enemy sowing weeds amid the good seeds. When the servants ask the master if they should weed the field, he responds, "No, lest in gathering the weeds you root up the wheat along with them. Let them grow together until the harvest" (13:29–30a). The tale is about the kingdom, with the wheat and the weeds being separated at the harvest and the wheat being gathered into the master's barn. But for me, the tale opened the way to a much deeper understanding of what Karla had said about evil. My normal human limitations make it impossible for me to weed out evil, which has nothing to do with God, without also weeding out what is good, which has everything to do with God. If I were to focus my thoughts and work on evil, therefore, I would sever links to God.

At first I was delighted with my insight. But suddenly I became sad and then felt myself slipping into a world of tragic loss. It seemed that one minute God was directing me toward a much more peaceful existence, and the next minute God was displaying before me an uncontained landscape of pain and suffering. Aware that I was in a precarious place, I prayed for deliverance. Soon I felt that I was returning to an allegedly more stable world, and I conveniently forgot about the morning's experience as I went on with my Sunday activities.

By the time I saw Karla again, that Sunday's experience seemed to be anchored in the past. It had lost a lot of its emotional energy, I noticed, as I described it to her. I remember her sitting quietly and contemplatively. I had seen her navigate through the sometimes Byzantine and often treacherous machinations of my parish church, and as I sat in her office that day, I was struck with a new perception about how she managed to carry on her work despite the environment. She did not engage with the bad stuff; she turned away from it and, so to speak, "Let the dead bury the dead."

As Karla sat very still, Buddha-like, I knew that she was turning away from a dialogue with me about evil.

In this final story from Ellen's spiritual direction, we can see not only her fluctuations of consolation and desolation within her narrative, but also the way she observes Karla's way of being in the parish and her way of being in spiritual direction. Ellen draws her own conclusions about how Karla embodies her insights about spiritual reality. Ellen assimilates not only Karla's eight words of wisdom, but also absorbs how she responds to a similar situation. In addition, Ellen uses scripture to interpret what she is seeing. We have no idea if Ellen's conclusions about Karla's approach to discernment and evil are accurate or not in terms of how Karla views her own situation. And we can also see how these two brief texts from scripture take on a completely new and particular meaning for Ellen.

* * *

We end this volume largely by how we began it, with a rich partial narrative of a directee's tale of spiritual direction. We highlighted, especially in this chapter, how the directee's narrative affects the director. He or she remains (or ought to remain) consciously interactive and mutually participative in the spiritual-direction conversation. If mutuality and reciprocity prevail in the spiritual-direction conversation, the compelling truth of the directee's life and actions addresses the director, and a new truth emerges for both. Because they both stand within similar or common faith traditions, the directee's story can become a contemporary form of "gospel" witness for the director, just as Ellen experiences such a witness in her director. Finally, the spiritual-direction situation can become a "sacramental" experience for the director as well as for the directee.

The sacred tale told in spiritual direction is never complete, always unfolding, and always susceptible to new interpretations and fresh revelations. In the twenty-first century, more than ever most of us can benefit from the opportunity to tell our sacred tale in spiritual direction for the sake of making sense out of our lives. Others write their sacred tales for the public on blogs and in autobiographies and memoirs. This process of discovering meaning through telling the stories of ourselves with God in various communities of faith is greatly enhanced by this public writing. Paul Elie writes:

> Believer and unbeliever are in the same predicament, thrown back onto themselves in complex circumstances, looking for a sign. As ever, religious belief makes its claim somewhere between revelation and projection, between holiness and human frailty; but the burden of proof, indeed the burden of belief, for so long upheld by society, is now back on the believer where it belongs.
>
> This is the significance of a piece of writing that makes a case for the Communion of Saints by way of one girl's short, hard, complicated life—and, perhaps, the significance of the religious faith that makes its case through the account of God's experience of life on earth as a certain person at a particular place and time. There is no way to seek truth except personally. Every story worth knowing is a life story....
>
> Like it or not, we come to life in the middle of stories that are not ours. The way to knowledge, and self-knowledge, is through pilgrimage. We imitate our way to the truth, finding our lives—saving them—in the process. Then we pass it on.
>
> The story of their lives, then, is also its meaning and its implication for ours. They saw religious experience out before them. They read their way toward it. They believed it. They lived it. They made it their own. With us in mind, they put it in writing.[13]

The writers whose work Elie explores in this volume and refers to above are Flannery O'Connor, Thomas Merton, Dorothy Day, and Walker Percy. Elie describes the significance for us of their storytelling. Those of us who live in a literate rather than oral culture read texts and see movies more than we hear stories being told to us. In our antimodern, modern, or postmodern context, we need to read, see, and hear such stories of belief and religious experience in our own cultures to nourish our sense of the Holy as being deeply involved with us. We need models for our own faith journeys, and yet we realize that each of us makes this journey both deeply alone and together with others in the Communion of Saints who have gone before us and who live among us in our faith communities.

In this ministry of spiritual direction, when we pay close attention to our directees' stories and to our own, we profoundly support one another on this journey of faith. Recently, in one of my workshops on narrative and spiritual direction, one director described our privileged role as spiritual directors who use a narrative mode: "As directors, we can discover ourselves as 'held' by a deep story from our tradition when we encounter experiences of directees that we don't understand. As directors we are not alone, but carry more stories than our own."

Thus, as directors, we are continually interacting among these three stories. Our own storied faith tradition holds us. We also incorporate a version of this deep story into our personal story in an ongoing dynamic process that is never finished. Finally, we receive our directees' personal stories and help them engage in a similar dynamic of reinterpreting their rich religious experience in dialogue with their own storied traditions. In this way, both we and they become educated in a wide range of alternative stories, and grow and change in the process.

Questions for Further Reflection

1. Do you notice how your directees' stories mediate grace to you?

2. How do you feel held by the stories of your own tradition?

3. How have you resolved conflicts of interpretation between you and your directees?

4. Have you learned to restrain your curiosity and to live with unfinished and ever changing narratives?

5. How have you helped directees make their own connections between sessions?

Notes

Introduction

1. William Johnston, trans., *The Cloud of Unknowing and the Book of Privy Counseling* (Garden City, NY: Doubleday, 1973), 182–83.

2. Tilden Edwards, *Spiritual Director/Spiritual Companion: Guide to Tending the Soul* (Mahwah, NJ: Paulist Press, 2001), 2–3.

3. Denis Edwards, *Human Experience of God* (New York: Paulist Press, 1983), 28; or Karl Rahner, *Foundations of Christian Faith* (New York: Seabury Press, 1978), 81–89.

4. Catherine Kohler Riessman, *Narrative Analysis*, Qualitative Research Methods Series 30 (Newbury Park, CA: 1993), 9.

5. Riessman, *Narrative Analysis*, 10–11.

6. For the history of spiritual direction, see Edouard des Places, "Direction Spirituelle," *Dictionnaire de Spiritualité*, vol. 3, cols. 1002–1214 (Paris: Beauchesne, 1980), hereafter cited as *DS*; and Kenneth Leech, *Soul Friend: The Practice of Christian Spirituality* (San Francisco: Harper and Row, 1980), 34–89. For a general treatment of the history of sacramental confession with relevance to spiritual guidance, see John T. McNeill, *A History of the Cure of Souls* (New York: Harper and Row, 1951); also Jerome Neufelder and Mary Coelho, eds., *Writings on Spiritual Direction by Great Christian Masters* (New York: Seabury Press, 1982). For essays (which originally appeared in *The Way*) on spiritual direction in relationship to historical schools of spirituality, see Lavinia Byrne, ed., *Traditions of Spiritual Guidance* (Collegeville, MN: Liturgical Press, 1990).

7. "The abba did not give 'spiritual direction'; if asked, he would give a 'word' which would become a sacrament to the hearer. The action of God was paramount and the only point of such 'words' was to free the disciple to be led by the Spirit of God, just as the abba himself would. In the desert there could only be one father to a disciple and even when he died, he was still the father of his sons. There was no need to change fathers, or to find a new one if one died. It was a lasting and permanent relationship. In such a relationship, tradition was passed on by life as well as by word; those

who had already been a certain way into the experience of the monastic life must be able to become this channel of grace to others. But the aim was always for the abba to disappear. The real guide was the Holy Spirit, who would be given to those who learned to receive him." Benedicta Ward, "Spiritual Direction in the Desert Fathers," *The Way* 24 (January 1984): 66.

8. "Spiritual Fatherhood in the Literature of the Desert," in John R. Sommerfeldt, ed., *Abba: Guides to Wholeness and Holiness, East and West* (Kalamazoo, MI: Cistercian Publications, 1982), 42.

9. Louf, in *Abba*, 45.

10. Ward, "Spiritual Direction in the Desert Fathers," 65.

11. "Charismatic" means that the person was accredited as a spiritual director by the Holy Spirit. Consequently, this task and responsibility of spiritual direction is a gift received from the Holy Spirit, in contrast to the institutional responsibility of an office such as ordination to the priesthood or the office of abbot/abbess.

12. *The Sayings of the Fathers*, in *Western Asceticism*, Owen Chadwick, trans. (Philadelphia: Westminster Press, 1958), records this anecdote: "An old man, who had a proved disciple, once turned him out in a fit of irritation. The disciple sat down outside to wait; and the old man found him there when he opened the door, and did penance to him, saying: 'You are my Father because your humility and patience have conquered the weakness of my soul. Come inside: now you are the old father, and I am the young disciple; my age must give way to your conduct'" (no. 17, 179).

13. Ward, "Spiritual Direction in the Desert Fathers," 65.

14. Chadwick, *The Sayings of the Fathers* (no. 10, 177).

15. See Michael Plattig and Regina Baumer for this emphasis, "The Desert Fathers and Spiritual Direction," *Studies in Spirituality* 7 (1997): 42–54.

16. Benedict of Nursia wrote his Rule sometime after 525 CE, while at Monte Cassino, Italy. This Rule formed the basis of life for the Benedictines and for the Cistercians (a reform dating from the late eleventh and twelfth centuries).

17. The relevant articles in the Rule are chapter 2, "The Qualities of the Abbot," and chapter 64, "The Election of an Abbot." See Timothy Fry, ed., *RB 1980: The Rule of St. Benedict in Latin and English with Notes* (Collegeville, MN: The Liturgical Press, 1981), hereafter cited as RB.

18. RB 7.44.

19. RB 58.6.

20. William of St. Thierry, *The Golden Epistle*, trans. Theodore Berkeley (Kalamazoo, MI: Cistercian Publications, 1980), no. 51. Also see nos. 53–54 and nos. 98–103 for further advice on the novice/spiritual-father relationship.

21. *The Golden Epistle*, no. 239.

22. William of St. Thierry, *Exposition on the Song of Songs*, trans. Mother Columba Hart (Shannon, Ireland: Irish University Press, 1969), no. 58.

23. The Fourth Lateran Council (1215) prescribed a rule of annual confession of sin for "every faithful of either sex who has reached the age of discretion...in secret to his own priest." Henricus Denzinger and Adolfus Schonmetzer, *Enchiridion Symbolorum*, 32nd ed. (Barcelona: Herder, 1963), no. 812. For the English translation see J. Neuner and J. Dupuis, eds., *The Christian Faith in the Doctrinal Documents of the Catholic Church*, rev. ed. (New York: Alba House, 1982), no. 1608.

24. The scope of the abbesses' spiritual leadership was extensive. "Women did exercise direct 'clerical' authority in the thirteenth century (preaching, hearing confessions from nuns under them, and bestowing blessings)....But such things were increasingly criticized and suppressed." Caroline Walker Bynum, *Jesus as Mother: Studies in the Spirituality of the High Middle Ages* (Berkeley: University of California Press, 1982), 15, 15n14, 16, 16n15.

25. Gordon S. Wakefield, ed., *The Westminster Dictionary of Christian Spirituality* (Louisville, KY: Westminster John Knox, 1983), s.v. "Dominican Spirituality, Dominicans," by Simon Tugwell.

26. "These were groups composed of women who chose...to set themselves apart from the world by living austere, poor lives in which manual labor and service were joined to worship....At least initially they contrasted sharply with traditional monasticism by taking no vows and having no complex organization and rules, no order linking the houses, no hierarchy of officials and no wealthy founders or leaders." Bynum, *Jesus as Mother*, 14.

27. "Direction Spirituelle," *DS*, vol. 3, col. 1083.

28. This was the name given to those women who adopted a non-monastic lifestyle, but who dedicated themselves totally to God.

29. Auguste Poulain defines supernatural ecstasy as "a state that not only at the outset, but during its whole existence, contains two essential elements: the first, which is interior and invisible, is a very intense attention to some religious subject; the second, which is corporeal and visible, is the alienation of the sensible faculties." *The Graces of Interior Prayer: A Treatise on Mystical Theology*, 6th ed. Leonora Smith, trans. (St. Louis: Herder, 1949), 243. Caroline Bynum adds that publicly observable ecstasy gave ecstatics "religious power" that competed with the power of office that clerics held. Through a eucharistic ecstasy they achieved "union with God in the central moment of mediation and thereby became mediators [of God] themselves. Thus they became...preachers, touchers of God, vessels within which God appeared." *Jesus as Mother*, 257–59.

30. Hadewijch of Antwerp, *Hadewijch: The Complete Works*, trans. Mother Columba Hart, Classics of Western Spirituality (New York: Paulist Press, 1980), 78.

31. Margery Kempe, *The Book of Margery Kempe*, ed. Sandford Meech and Hope Allen (Oxford: Oxford University Press, 1961), 42.

32. Kenelm Foster and Mary John Ronayne, eds. and trans., *I, Catherine: Selected Writings of St. Catherine of Siena* (London: Collins, 1980), 15.

33. Hadewijch's writings consisted of letters, poems in stanzas, visions, and poems in couplets, compiled in *The Complete Works*. Julian of Norwich wrote *Showings*, intro. and trans. Edmund Colledge and James Walsh, Classics of Western Spirituality (New York: Paulist Press, 1978). Catherine of Siena dictated *The Dialogue* to Raymond of Capua, her secretary; see *Catherine of Siena: The Dialogue*, intro. and trans. Suzanne Noffke, Classics of Western Spirituality (New York: Paulist Press, 1980). For Catherine's letters, see Le *Lettere di s. Caterina da Siena*, ed. P. Misciatelli, 4 vols. (Florence: G. Barbera, 1860); also *The Letters of St. Catherine of Siena*, vols. 1 and 2, trans. Suzanne Noffke (Tempe, AZ: Medieval and Renaissance Texts and Studies, 2000). Catherine of Genoa's teaching was compiled by her disciple Ettore Vernazza after her death; see *Catherine of Genoa: Purgation and Purgatory, The Spiritual Dialogue*, trans. Serge Hughes, intro. Benedict Groeschel (New York: Paulist Press, 1979).

34. Thomas of Cantimpré, the Dominican prior of Louvain, referred to St. Lutgard of Aywiéres (d. 1246) as his *mater specialissima*, and James of Vitry "regularly calls Mary of Oignies (d. 1213) his *mater spiritualis.*" Paul Mommaers, "Hadewijch: A Feminist in Conflict," Louvain Studies 13 (1988), 21.

35. Gerard J. Campbell briefly describes the structure and process of these exercises: "The First Week is preceded by a kind of preamble called First Principle and Foundation. This is a consideration concerning creation, the purpose of life, and the proper relationship of a person to the rest of creation. The First Week is devoted to prayer about sin and its consequences. The Second Week begins with a contemplation of Christ's kingship over the world. There follows a series of contemplations on the mysteries of Christ's life up to the Last Supper. During this week various exercises are proposed to assist the retreatant to make choices about the direction of his or her life or about a better fulfillment of choices already made. The Third Week brings the retreatant to share in the sufferings and death of Jesus and to appreciate his saving love in the passion. Finally the Fourth Week leads the retreatant to an experience of the joy Jesus shared with his followers in his risen life. The concluding exercise is a profound and intimate experience of the many gifts of God's love to the individual and an invitation to an appro-

priate response of love in return." *The Westminster Dictionary*, s.v. "The Spiritual Exercises."

36. Ignatius of Loyola, *The Spiritual Exercises*, trans. Louis J. Puhl (Chicago: Loyola University Press, 1951), no 1.

37. Puhl, *Spiritual Exercises*, no. 20.

38. Ignatius of Loyola, *The Spiritual Exercises of St. Ignatius of Loyola with a Commentary and "Directorium in Exercitia,"* trans. W. H. Longridge (London: Roxburgh House, 1919).

39. Ignatius's term for the one who makes the Exercises.

40. Puhl, *Spiritual Exercises*, no. 18.

41. Puhl, *Spiritual Exercises*, no. 4. See also supplementary information on these points in the *Directory on the Exercises*, chapters 2, 5, 8, and 9, cited above in note 38.

42. Puhl, *Spiritual Exercises*, nos. 7–11. Ernest Larkin describes discernment of spirits this way: "It [discernment] seeks to read the movements of the sensible and spiritual affectivity in a positive way, i.e., as signs of the influence of the Spirit or a counterforce. This is possible in the Second Week, because the affectivity now registers in an immediate, uncensored way the reaction of the whole person. Specifically the feelings now show the consonance or dissonance between the present experience and the spiritual orientation of the person. The criteriology of these affective responses is precisely the tradition of discernment." *The Westminster Dictionary*, s.v. "Discernment of Spirits."

43. Puhl, *Spiritual Exercises*, nos. 4 and 18.

44. Puhl, *Spiritual Exercises*, nos. 2 and 15.

45. Puhl, *Spiritual Exercises*, no. 17. See also the *Directory* in note 38, above, chapters 7 and 2.7.

46. See Joseph de Guibert, *The Jesuits: Their Spiritual Doctrine and Practice*, trans. William J. Young from the 1953 ed. (Chicago: Institute of Jesuit Sources, 1964), 3, 10–11.

47. See especially Kathryn Dyckman, Mary Garvin, and Elizabeth Liebert's *The Spiritual Exercises Reclaimed: Uncovering Liberating Possibilities for Women* (Mahwah, NJ: Paulist Press, 2001) for helpful and necessary adaptations for women making or giving the Exercises.

48. This ecumenical council was primarily concerned with elaborating the Catholic response to the challenge of the Protestant Reformation.

49. "Ask your spiritual director to prescribe your acts of devotion, for this will double their value and merit; for over and above their intrinsic value, Philothea, they will have the merit of being done under obedience." Francis De Sales, *Introduction to the Devout Life*, trans. Michael Day (Westminster, MD: Newman Press, 1956), 122.

50. Thomas Merton, "The Spiritual Father in the Desert Tradition," in *Contemplation in a World of Action* (Garden City, NY: Doubleday, 1965), 282.

51. Leech, *Soul Friend*, 58.

52. "God, who established His Church as a hierarchical society, has willed that souls be sanctified through submission to the Sovereign Pontiff and to the Bishops in things external, and to confessors in things internal....[The duties of penitents flow from this same view of authority:] Penitents will see in their spiritual director the person of Our Lord Himself. If it is true that all authority comes from God, it is more so of the authority the priest exercises over consciences in the confessional. The power of binding and loosing, of opening and closing the gates of heaven, of guiding souls in the paths of perfection, is a divine power and cannot reside outside him who is the lawful representative, the ambassador of Christ....This is the principle from which all duties toward a spiritual director flow— respect, trust, docility." Adolphe Tanquerey, *The Spiritual Life: A Treatise on Ascetical and Mystical Theology*, trans. Herman Branderis (Westminster, MD: Newman Press, 1930), nos. 531, 551.

53. "Listen to him, then, as though he were an angel from heaven sent to guide you there." De Sales, *The Devout Life*, 16.

54. "Some souls do see their way before them far better than others, and therefore do move fewer questions. The instructor therefore is to...instruct his disciples how they may themselves find out the way proper for them, by observing themselves what doeth good and what causeth harm to their spirits; in a word, that he is only God's usher." Dom Augustine Baker, *Holy Wisdom* (London: Burns Oates, 1911), no. 27. See John of the Cross, *Living Flame of Love*, chapter 3, nos. 30–62, in *The Collected Works of St. John of the Cross*, trans. Kieran Kavanaugh and Otilio Rodriguez (Washington, DC: ICS Publications, 1973), for a description of the role of the director and the harm done by incompetence. Also see chapters 4, 13, 29, and elsewhere in *The Life of Teresa of Jesus*, trans. E. Allison Peers (Garden City, NY: Doubleday, 1960), for her comments about spiritual directors.

55. Tanquerey, *The Spiritual Life*, 11. This manual of ascetical and mystical theology represented the culmination of this whole approach to the spiritual life from the sixteenth century to the first part of the twentieth century.

56. Tanquerey, *The Spiritual Life*, 22–23.

57. Tanquerey, *The Spiritual Life*, 22, 270.

58. Thérèse of Lisieux, *Story of a Soul*, trans. John Clarke (Washington, DC: ICS Publications, 1976), 150–51.

59. "A man of wide experience, Father Desurmont, writes as follows on [directing women:] 'Let there be nothing savoring of feel-

ing, either in manner or gesture, nor the least shadow of familiarity. As to conversations, no more than is necessary; as to dealings outside of matters of conscience, only those that have a recognized serious purpose. As much as possible, let there be no direction outside the confessional, and no correspondence. They must not be made even to suspect that one is personally interested in them. Their mentality is so constituted that if they be led to think themselves the object of a particular regard or affection, almost without fail, they descend to a natural plane, be it through vanity or sentimentality.'" Tanquerey, *The Spiritual Life*, no. 546c, 265.

60. Despite the domination of this post-Tridentine model of confining spiritual direction to the confessional, there were some notable exceptions. See Patricia Ranft, *A Woman's Way: The Forgotten History of Women Spiritual Directors* (New York: Palgrave, 2000), 107–56. Ranft describes the spiritual direction given by Jane Frances De Chantal, Louise de Marillac, Angela Merici, Mary Ward, and Teresa of Avila. In addition, there were also notable non-ordained men such as Brother Gerard Magellan, a Redemptorist, and Holy Cross Brother Andre in Montreal—both of whom were assigned to answering the door of their monasteries and became recognized for their extraordinary gifts of spiritual direction.

61. The titles of books on spiritual direction reflect this concern for acceptable images, especially in non–Roman Catholic circles. See Leech, *Soul Friend*; Tilden Edwards, *Spiritual Friend: Reclaiming the Gift of Spiritual Direction* (New York: Paulist Press, 1980) and, more recently, his *Spiritual Director/Spiritual Companion* (2001); Jeannette Bakke, *Holy Invitations: Exploring Spiritual Direction* (Grand Rapids: Baker Books, 2000); and Margaret Guenther's *Holy Listening* (Cambridge, MA: Cowley, 1992).

62. Sandra Schneiders and Nemeck and Coombs exemplify attempts to redefine the terminology in an acceptable way. "Spiritual direction can be understood as a process, carried out in a one-to-one interpersonal context, of establishing and maintaining a growth orientation (that is, direction) in one's faith life. This process has two moments which are in constant dialectical relationship with each other, namely, listening to and articulating God's call in one's life, and progressively elaborating an integrated and adequate response to that call." Schneiders, "The Contemporary Ministry of Spiritual Direction," *Chicago Studies* 15 (Spring 1976): 123. Likewise, Francis Kelly Nemeck and Marie Theresa Coombs assert, "The spiritual director...helps bring into consciousness and explicate the already existing spiritual direction in which the Spirit is leading the directee." Nemeck and Coombs, *The Way of Spiritual Direction* (Wilmington, DE: Michael Glazier, 1985), 31. Jeannette Bakke retains this terminology in an evangelical context, "because a vast body of

literature can be explored most easily by using this term; *Holy Invitations*, 18ff.

63. See Edwards, *Spiritual Director*, 21–3, for his assessment that spiritual direction is not a passing fad and for his description of factors contributing to the growth of spiritual direction from a Protestant perspective.

64. See Sandra M. Schneiders, "Horizons on Spiritual Direction," *Horizons* 11 (Spring 1984): 100–111 for a review of the early books on this subject. See my "Review Essay: Recent Literature and Emerging Trends in Spiritual Direction," *Spiritus: The Journal of the Society for the Study of Christian Spirituality* 3 (Spring 2002): 99–107, for important contributions to the field since 1995. See also various essays in *Presence: An International Journal of Spiritual Direction*.

65. Two other definitions of spiritual direction in the contemporary context emphasize different aspects. William A. Barry and William J. Connolly offer an experiential definition: "We define Christian spiritual direction, then, as help given by one Christian to another which enables that person to pay attention to God's personal communication to him or her, to respond to this personally communicating God, to grow in intimacy with this God, and to live out the consequences of the relationship." See *The Practice of Spiritual Direction* (New York: Seabury Press, 1982), 8. Sandra M. Schneiders further defines direction as "a process carried out in the context of a one-to-one relationship in which a competent guide helps a fellow Christian to grow in the spiritual life by means of personal encounters that have the directee's spiritual growth as their explicit object," in "Contemporary Ministry," 124.

66. See Bruce H. Lescher, "Catholicism and Postmodernity: Faithing Our Practice," *The Way* 41 (July 2001): 252–53.

67. Robert F. Morneau described the spiritual director as a literary critic, using this term only as a metaphor rather than identifying the directee's telling his or her sacred story as a core feature of spiritual direction. Since the first edition of this book, there has been little explicit attention given to narrative in spiritual direction. "The Spiritual Director as Literary Critic," *Review for Religious* (March/April 1985): 220–32.

Chapter 1

1. Both Sam and Mary wrote their case studies for inclusion in this book, reconstructing the events from memory. Sam wrote his narrative during the fall following the year's experience in spiritual

direction recorded in his case. Mary wrote hers three years after the retreat she describes. Usually case studies are written from the point of view of the spiritual director or counselor. Because Sam and Mary, as well as many other people cited in this text, wrote their stories of spiritual direction, we hear accounts of spiritual direction from the point of view of directees rather than of directors. This respects them, leaving them free to disclose what they feel comfortable saying about their lives and their experience of spiritual direction. Had their directors written these cases, a different story from a different perspective is likely. Sam knew about my interest in narrative in spiritual direction, but had not read anything I had written about narrative and spiritual direction before writing his story. Mary, on the other hand, had read chapters from the first edition of this book. In order to protect their confidentiality, I have given pseudonyms to them and anyone else mentioned in their case studies. Sam's account of spiritual direction represents his experience of ongoing spiritual direction, while Mary's sacred tale is about a retreat experience with a different spiritual director. In Mary's story, the director pays a lot of attention to her emotional issues because she was so raw from her recent divorce. He responds less explicitly to the narrative details embedded in her story. Consequently, the reader may sense the contrast between a narrative approach to spiritual direction and a more psychological approach.

2. Castro Street is the center of a gay neighborhood in San Francisco, recently portrayed in the film *Milk*.

3. As I reflected with Mary, long after this retreat, we both felt that responses to the specific images emerging in her narrative might have better supported her growth than her director's suggesting new images or projecting a line of development in her relationship with God not yet in her awareness. From her narrative of her retreat, it is often difficult to know whether or not Mary told her director about a given experience in prayer when she also brings up another topic she needed to discuss. Consequently, when I reflect on this case material, I am relying on what Mary told me. Her director may well have been responding to a different version of Mary's story, as well as to more of her life story and prayer experience heard from previous retreats. Thus, my intention is not to critique another spiritual director's work from this partial perspective; rather, I hope to suggest an expanded repertoire of possible responses that might have followed from Mary's own story.

Chapter 2

1. Scott Holland, *How Do Stories Save Us? An Essay on the Question with the Theological Hermeneutics of David Tracy in View*, Louvain Theological and Pastoral Monographs 35 (Leuven, Belgium: Peeters / W. B. Eerdmans, 2006).

2. Hans-Georg Gadamer, *Truth and Method*, trans. and ed. Garrett Barden and John Cumming from the 1965 ed. (New York: Crossroad, 1975), 340.

3. Gadamer, *Truth and Method*, 248.

4. Gadamer, *Truth and Method*, 330–31.

5. Gadamer, *Truth and Method*, 249–51.

6. For an excellent overview of current understanding of how narrative relates to theology, see Scott Holland, *How Do Stories Save Us?* especially the chapters "How Do Stories Save?" 71–104, and "Theology Is a Kind of Writing," 105–32. For an accessible description of the reasons for the development of narrative theology in the United States, see Terrence W. Tilley, *Story Theology*, Theology and Life Series 12 (Collegeville, MN: Liturgical Press, 1985), 18–36, 39–53, for a lucid description of the necessary shapes of stories needed for story theology and for Christian living.

7. Tilley emphasizes that three specific types of stories are required for this process. "A narrative theology of myth [world-creating stories] without parable would be stifling; of parable [stories that upset worlds] without myth would be baffling; of action alone [stories that reveal how things work in a world] would be boring. Narrative theology must attend to all the types of stories." *Story Theology*, 53.

8. Tilley has expanded his view about the genres of stories that might achieve the three functions described above. He now claims that sagas are equally world-creating stories as myth, and he cites theologian Roberto Goizueta's use of Passion Week stories as combining action stories and ritualized world-making narrative. Tilley also points to neglected stories of marginalized people, such as stories about Our Lady of Guadalupe, as working equally well as myth to upset the world of the conquistadores, who imposed their discourse on a conquered people. "Experience and Narrative," in *Tradition and Pluralism: Essays in Honor of William M. Shea*, ed. Kenneth L. Parker, Peter A. Huff, and Michael J. G. Pahls, Studies in Religion and the Social Order (Lanham, MD: Univ. Press of America, 2009), 16. In this more recent reflection, Tilley encourages us to expand our storytelling beyond the more personal and autobiographical story to embrace "the narratives of our communities and our praxis." He points out that "our stories are not about us; we are characters in our stories. Nor are they about our communities; our

communities are contexts for and creations of our stories. Nor are they merely about our actions; though the stories are of actions we participate in, undertake, and suffer....[Even more important,] our stories are about...God's dealing with our community, with me, with our work, with our praxis. They are about grace in the concrete, God in the quotidian." Tilley, "Experience and Narrative," 17.

9. Robert Alter, *The Art of Biblical Narrative* (New York: Basic Books, 1981), 4.

10. Eric Auerbach claims that biblical narrative influenced the Western literary tradition in the direction of realism. On the other hand, a non-Christian literary form, the journey, was adopted and adapted by Augustine to create the confessional form. Later forms of autobiography eventually abandoned a spiritual purpose. *Mimesis: The Representation of Reality in Western Literature*, trans. Willard R. Trask (Princeton: Princeton Univ. Press, 1953).

11. Auerbach, *Mimesis*, 62.

12. Gadamer, *Truth and Method*, 269.

13. Gadamer, *Truth and Method*, 269–72.

14. Barret J. Mandel, "Full of Life Now," in *Autobiography: Theoretical and Critical*, ed. James Olney (Princeton: Princeton Univ. Press, 1980), 68–69.

15. Gadamer, *Truth and Method*, 261.

16. Gadamer, *Truth and Method*, 261.

17. Feminist scholarship has continued to develop for many years now, having moved from an intense period of critique of patriarchal erasure of women from history, to a historical retrieval of women's history in Christian tradition in biblical and historical studies, which still continues, and to creative constructive feminist theology and spirituality. See the Madeleva Lecture Series for a great variety of these topics; the lectures have all been published by Paulist Press for the last twenty-five years. See also, among others, the biblical work of Elisabeth Schüssler Fiorenza and Sandra Schneiders; the theological and historical work of Rosemary Radford Reuther; the theological work of Elisabeth Johnson, Ann Carr, and Catherine La Cugna; and the spirituality work by Elizabeth Dreyer and Beverly Lanzetta.

18. Gadamer, *Truth and Method*, 278.

19. For Gadamer's treatment of Aristotle, see *Truth and Method*, 278–89.

20. Gadamer, *Truth and Method*, 288.

21. Psychologist Carl Rogers offers this definition of empathy: "The state of empathy or being empathic is to perceive the internal frame of reference of another with accuracy and with the emotional components and meanings which pertain thereto, as if one were the other person but without ever losing the 'as if' condition. Thus it

means to sense the hurt or the pleasure of another as he/she senses it, and to perceive the causes thereof as he/she perceives them, but without ever losing the recognition that it is 'as if' we were hurt or pleased, etc. If this 'as if' quality is lost, then the state is one of identification." *Client-Centered Therapy* (Boston: Houghton Mifflin, 1959), 210–11. Psychologist Beverly Musgrave emphasizes that the empathic person not only "attempts to enter the world of another, to understand the other and to feel with the other," but also does so, "while remaining a differentiated person." Beverly Musgrave, "Relatedness: Sexuality and Intimacy," in *The Family and Contemporary Social Realty: Pastoral Priorities and Challenges*, Proceedings of the Seminar for Bishops Chairmen: Commission on the Family in the Countries of Asia (Chennai, India: SERFAC, 1999), 107.

22. David Tracy, *Blessed Rage for Order: The New Pluralism in Theology* (Chicago: Univ. of Chicago Press, 1996), 105.

23. Holland, speaking about Tracy, *How Do Stories Save Us?* 52.

24. Holland, speaking about Tracy, *How Do Stories Save Us?* 54.

25. Tracy, *Blessed Rage*, 136.

26. Johann Baptist Metz, *Passion for God: The Mystical-Political Dimension of Christianity*, trans. Matthew Ashley (Mahwah, NJ: Paulist Press, 1998), 103.

27. Metz, *Passion for God*, 102.

28. David Tracy, *On Naming the Present: Reflections on God, Hermeneutics, and Church* (Maryknoll, NY: Orbis, 1994), 3–4. The title chapter was originally published in *Concilium* 1990/1.

29. Tracy, *On Naming the Present*, 4.

30. Tracy, *On Naming the Present*, 4.

31. Tracy, *On Naming the Present*, 4–5.

32. Tracy, *On Naming the Present*, 5–6.

33. Tracy, *On Naming the Present*, 21–22; he quotes Gutiérrez in the next line on page 22.

34. Tracy, *On Naming the Present*, 22.

35. Tracy, *On Naming the Present*, 43.

36. Tracy, *On Naming the Present*, 44.

37. Tracy, *On Naming the Present*, 45.

Chapter 3

1. Jill Freedman and Gene Combs, *Narrative Therapy: The Social Construction of Preferred Realities* (New York: Norton, 1996); J. Lenore Wright, *The Philosopher's "I": Autobiography and the Search for Self* (Albany: SUNY Press, 2006).

2. D. Jean Clandinin and F. Michael Connelly, *Narrative*

Inquiry: Experience and Story in Qualitative Research (San Francisco: Jossey-Bass, 2000). Elizabeth McIsaac Bruce, "Narrative Inquiry: A Spiritual and Liberating Approach to Research," *Religious Education* 103/3 (2008): 323–38; downloaded by EBSCO *host* EJS at Fordham University Library on September 18, 2008. Martin Kreiswirth, "Trusting the Tale: The Narrativist Turn in the Human Sciences," *New Literary History* 23/3 (Summer 1992): 629–57; accessed from http://www/jstor.org/stable/469223 on February 2, 2009 at Fordham University Library. Peggy J. Miller, Randolph Potts, Heidi Fung, Lisa Hoogstra, and Judy Mintz, "Narrative Practices and the Social Construction of the Self in Childhood," *American Ethnologist* 17/2 (May 1990): 292–311; downloaded from E-Journals at Fordham University Library on February 13, 2009. Jerome Bruner, "The Autobiographical Process," in *The Culture of Autobiography: Constructions of Self-Representation*, ed. Robert Folkenflik (Palo Alto, CA: Stanford University Press, 1993).

3. See, for instance, Paul John Eakin, *How Our Lives Become Stories: Making Selves* (Ithaca, NY: Cornell University Press, 1999), and Paul John Eakin, ed., *The Ethics of Life Writing* (Ithaca, NY: Cornell University Press, 2004). Sidonie Smith and Julia Watson, eds., *Women, Autobiography, Theory: A Reader* (Madison: University of Wisconsin Press, 1998). Rosamund Dalziell, ed., *Selves Crossing Cultures: Autobiography and Globalisation* (Melbourne: Australian Scholarly Publishing, 2002). Mary Besemeres, *Translating One's Self: Language and Selfhood in Cross-Cultural Autobiography* (Oxford: Peter Lang, 2002). David Parker, "Inhabiting Multiple Worlds: Auto/biography in an (Anti-)Global Age," *Biography* 28.1 (2005): v–xv; accessed online through Project Muse, Fordham University Library on March 11, 2009. And finally, Thomas Albrecht and Celine Suprenant, "The Year's Work in Critical and Cultural Theory," *Narrative* 14 (2006): 89–117; this review essay shows the expansion of narrative theory to media studies, for instance, defining narrative beyond linguistic categories to include by definition, minimally, "dimensions of space (a world, characters, objects), time (changes of state), and plot (causal relations, motivations)," 91. The essay also shows a second way of categorizing narrative that is based on the medium: "face-to-face narration (which is to say storytelling), still pictures, moving pictures, music and digital media," 93. Downloaded from http://proquest.umi.com/dqwebindex=96&did1141213091&Srch Mode=1&sid=1&Fm at Fordham University Library on October 26, 2007.

4. "There are two modes of cognitive functioning, two modes of thought, each providing distinctive ways of ordering experience, of constructing reality. The two (though complementary) are irreducible to one another. Efforts to reduce one mode to the other or

to ignore one at the expense of the other inevitably fail to capture the rich diversity of thought....A good story and a well-formed argument are different natural kinds. Both can be used as a means for convincing another. Yet what they convince of is fundamentally different." Bruner, cited by Martin Kreiswirth, "Trusting the Tale," 650; for the full reference, see above, note 2, chapter 3.

5. Clandinin and Connelly, *Narrative Inquiry*, 17.

6. Barbara Herrnstein Smith says that every narration is created in relationship to the interrelated factors of (1) a concrete teller, (2) an occasion for the telling, and (3) the purposes, perceptions, actions, or interactions that occur in the face-to-face situation. "Narrative Versions, Narrative Theories," in *On Narrative*, ed. W. T. J. Mitchell (Chicago: University of Chicago Press, 1981), 217, 222.

7. Telling one's sacred tale does not exclude all other forms of speech in spiritual direction. However, the directee's life story does provide a major context for interpreting other forms of speech, such as meditation, doxology, theological reflection, and lyric poetry, or for sharing insights that arise from intuitive, contemplative perceptions.

8. The terms *narrative* and *story* will usually be used interchangeably, although some literary critics make a distinction between them.

9. Philosopher Paul Ricoeur describes two of the most important features of all narrative as "sequence and pattern," or a combination of a chronological dimension with one that is not. The dimension of pattern creates "significant wholes out of scattered events." This patterning accomplished in the telling of a story or a series of related events adds the reflective judgment of the narrator to the storytelling. "To tell and to follow a story is already to reflect upon events in order to encompass them in successive wholes." Ricoeur, "The Narrative Function," *Semeia* 13 (1978): 183–85. For Ricoeur's extended analysis of emplotment, see *Time and Myth*, vol. 1, trans. Kathleen McLaughlin and David Pellauer (Chicago: University of Chicago Press, 1983), 31–51.

10. Clandinin and Connelly in *Narrative Inquiry* cite Donald Polkinghorne's assessment that narrative inquiry can be either descriptive or explanatory. Descriptive narratives represent accurately "the interpretive narrative accounts [that] individuals or groups use to make sequences of events in their lives...meaningful." Explanatory narratives account for "the connection between events in a causal sense...and to supply the connections," 16.

11. See Robert Scholes and Robert Kellogg, *The Nature of Narrative* (New York: Harper, 1966), chapter 7; and Wayne C. Booth, *The Rhetoric of Fiction*, 2nd ed. (Chicago: University of Chicago Press, 1983), chapters 7–10.

12. Northrop Frye describes this as "explanation by emplotment." *Anatomy of Criticism* (Princeton: Princeton University Press, 1981), 353–54.

13. Paul Ricoeur describes this relationship between explanation and plot for writing history: "The historian...does not merely tell a story. He makes an entire set of events, considered as a whole, into a story." In "The Narrative Function," 189.

14. James Hillman, *Healing Fiction* (Barrytown, NY: Station Hill, 1983), 9–10. There has been an extensive development in psychoanalytic circles that analysis, as Martin Kreiswirth states, "is now unabashedly acclaimed, both in its theory and clinical practice, as a narrative activity, pure and simple." "The Narrativist Turn in the Human Sciences," 647. Francoise Meltzer puts it this way: "The very process of psychoanalysis entails the construction of a linear, cogent narrative; the recounting and piecing together of a life. The goal of analysis is to have the patient reconstruct a 'better,' more coherent story as the analysis progresses. The analysis is narrative, and the analysand is the narrator. The analyst, it follows, assumes the role of the reader of this narrative, for he or she is obliged...to reconstruct in turn the 'plot' of a life as it is itself being constructed. And too, the analyst must 'read' the 'subplot' of this narrative: the unconscious as it may be itself reconstructed from the disguises and displacements it assumes in the tale the patient tells....[The analyst] plays the role not only of reader but also of critic. For the analyst must first 'read' or interpret the narrative. Then he or she must persuade the analysand of the accuracy of his or her own, corrected version and interpretation." Cited by Kreiswirth, "The Narrativist Turn," 647–88. Also the following sources by Freudian analyst Roy Schafer: "Listening in Psychoanalysis," *Narrative* 13.3 (2005): 271–80; "Narrating, Attending, and Empathizing," *Literature and Medicine* 23.2 (2004): 241–51, and Schafer's own reformulation of his initial considerations on analysis as narrative, *Retelling a Life: Narration and Dialogue in Psychoanalysis* (New York: Basic Books, 1992).

15. Ricoeur, "Narrative Function," 182.

16. Michael Novak, *Ascent of the Mountain, Flight of the Dove* (San Francisco: Harper and Row, 1971), 49.

17. Stephen Crites, "The Narrative Quality of Experience," *The Journal of the American Academy of Religion* 39 (September 1971): 291–97.

18. Crites, "The Narrative Quality," 291.

19. Three specific practices affect young children in teaching them how to tell their stories: mothers or primary caregivers tell stories about the child in the child's presence to a third person, they intervene in the child's attempt to tell a personal story, and the child

appropriates others' stories. In this ethnographical study, the authors also assume that telling personal stories in face-to-face situations is a cultural universal, that narrative plays a privileged role in the process of self-construction because of the relationship between time and narrative, the psychological need for self-continuity, and narrative's capacity for representing human action (292). Peggy J. Miller, Randolph Potts, Heidi Fung, Lisa Hoogstra, and Judy Mintz, "Narrative Practices in the Social Construction of Self in Childhood," *American Ethnologist* 17/2 (May 1990): 292–311.

20. Crites, "Narrative Quality," 292.

21. Crites, "Narrative Quality," 294.

22. Terrence Tilley, "Experience and Narrative" in *Tradition and Pluralism: Essays in Honor of William M. Shea*, eds. Kenneth L. Parker, Peter A. Huff, and Michael J. G. Pahls (Lanham, MD: University Press of America, 2009), 16.

23. See Crites, "Narrative Quality," 295–97, for his development of this theme.

24. Crites, "Narrative Quality," 294–97.

25. Crites, "Narrative Quality," 294–97.

26. The next chapter will describe new understandings of the autobiographical self and the core self that have developed in relationship to the discoveries of neuroscientists in understanding how the brain actually reconstructs all types of memory. Crites's reflection in which he contrasts "recall" from one's chronological image stream with "recollection," as the term he uses for recreating a fuller memory of an event in a more complex way, is based on phenomenological reflection of what it feels like to remember a key event, but which we now know is neurologically even more complex. I now rely on Antonio Damasio's account of consciousness that includes a proto-self, a core self, and the autobiographical self; a consciousness that creates a single sense of self from this complex brain activity and descriptions of, what Ulric Neisser calls, "registers of the self." Antonio Damasio, *The Feeling of What Happens: Body and Emotion in the Making of Consciousness* (New York: Harcourt, 1999), especially chapters 6 and 7 on the core self and the extended self. Ulric Neisser, "Five Kinds of Self-Knowledge," *Philosophical Psychology* 1 (1988): 35–59, accessed online, academic Google, March 16, 2009. Also see Neisser with Robyn Fivush, *The Remembering Self: Construction and Accuracy in the Self-Narrative* (New York: Cambridge University Press, 1994).

27. Crites, "Narrative Quality," 300–301.

28. Hans-Georg Gadamer contrasts dynamic memory with "retention." Retention corresponds to Crites's description of simple recall. Gadamer says, "Remembering, forgetting, and recalling belong to the historical constitution of man [*sic*] and are themselves

part of his history....Memory must be formed; for memory is not memory for anything and everything. One has a memory for many things, and not for others; one wants to preserve one thing in memory and banish another....Forgetting belongs within the context of remembering and recalling in a way that has long been ignored; forgetting is not merely an absence and a lack but...a condition of the life of mind. Only by forgetting does the mind have the chance of total renewal, the capacity to see everything with fresh eyes, so that what is long familiar combines with the new into a many leveled unity." *Truth and Method*, trans. and ed. Garrett Barden and John Cumming from the 1965 ed. (New York: Crossroad, 1975), 16.

29. Gadamer also reflects on the dialectical nature of new experience to confound our expectations that we know what to expect of someone or something. "We use the word 'experience' in two different senses: to refer to the experiences that fit in with our expectations and confirm it, and to the experience we have. This latter, 'experience' in the real sense, is always negative. If we have an experience of an object, this means that we have not seen the thing correctly hitherto and now know it better." *Truth and Method*, 317. Thus, a new experience is always disconfirming of expectations, and challenges us not to force it to fit into old categories.

30. Others develop the importance of embodiment more completely than does Crites. For instance, Jerry H. Gill, drawing on phenomenologist Merleau-Ponty's work, says, "Our bodies serve as the juncture at which we interact with and affect our world. We move toward and into our world through our bodies, just as it moves toward and engages us through our bodies. For the obvious but nonetheless amazing fact is that our bodies are both us and part of the world. Our existence is constituted by them and their existence is constituted by the world." Gill, *On Knowing God* (Philadelphia: Westminster Press, 1981), 70–71. See also, John Giles Milhaven, *Hadewijch and Her Sisters: Other Ways of Knowing and Loving* (Albany: SUNY Press, 1993), for an account of embodied knowing and loving in women mystics especially. He argues against the sense of sight as the preferred metaphor for knowing in Western philosophy, and for the more intimate senses of touch, taste, and so on, of family and sexual life.

31. This less cohesive form of consciousness has frequently been represented in literature using the technique called "stream of consciousness," which reconstructs a more fragmented focus of attention in which sensations, thoughts, and feelings interpose themselves between the events of the plot. Although this form of consciousness does not organize itself into a single unified story with all of the details relating to the main narrative line, it is still organized at least by the temporal succession of before and after.

32. Novak, *Ascent of the Mountain*, 9. Novak also notes that the more mainstream we might be, the more likely we may not even realize that we have a story. We are just like everyone else we know and are pretty well mirrored by normative stories of our culture.

33. Denis Edwards, *The Human Experience of God* (New York: Paulist Press, 1983), 7.

34. Edwards, *The Human Experience of God*, 7.

35. Edward Schillebeeckx, *Christ: The Experience of Jesus as Lord*, trans. John Bowden (New York: Crossroad, 1981), 33.

36. In this section, *preconceptual* corresponds to the tacit or skill dimension as Michael Polanyi defines it in *Personal Knowledge: Towards a Post-Critical Philosophy* (Chicago: University of Chicago Press, 1958). As an epistemological concept, *preconceptual* is not entirely synonymous with Gadamer's term *prejudice*.

37. "Although the expert diagnostician, taxonomist and cotton-classer can indicate their clues and formulate their maxims, they know many more things than they can tell, knowing them only in practice, as instrumental particulars, and not explicitly as objects." Polanyi, *Personal Knowledge*, 88.

38. Schillebeeckx describes the interrelationship between "objective" and "subjective" elements in experience in this way: "Our real experiences are neither purely objective nor purely subjective. At least partially, there is something which is 'given,' which we cannot completely manipulate or change; in experience we have an offer of reality. On the other hand, it is not purely objective; for the experience is filled out and colored by the reminiscences and sensibilities, concepts and longings of the person who has the experience. Thus the irreducible elements of our experiences form a totality which already contains interpretation. We experience in the act of interpreting, without being able to draw a neat distinction between the element of experience and the element of interpretation." Schillebeeckx, *Christ*, 33.

39. This persuasive function of narrative leads to its rhetorical character. George A. Kennedy describes rhetoric: "Rhetoric is a form of communication. The author of a communication has some kind of purpose, and rhetoric certainly includes the ways by which he seeks to accomplish that purpose....Purposes cover a whole spectrum from converting hearers to a view opposed to that they previously held, to implanting a conviction not otherwise considered, to deepening belief in a view already favorably entertained, to a demonstration of the cleverness of the author, to teaching or exposition. In practice almost every communication is rhetorical in that it uses some device to try to affect the thought, actions, or emotions of an audience, but the degree of rhetoric varies enormously." *Classical Rhetoric and Its Christian and Secular Tradition from*

Ancient to Modern Times (Chapel Hill, NC: University of North Carolina Press, 1980), 4. Directees employ rhetoric consciously and unconsciously in the spiritual direction dialogue as we do in any form of communication. Directees want the director to find their stories plausible and convincing, and will shape their narratives to include what a director shows interest in. It is even not unusual for a directee to tell his or her sacred tale in a lively and entertaining way, especially if the core event is problematic or painful. If, however, a directee is unable to moderate attempts to persuade the director that his or her narrative interpretation of an experience is the only possible way that the event can be understood, the process of spiritual direction may be frustrated.

40. William J. Bausch, *Touching the Heart: Tales for the Human Journey* (New London, CT: Twenty-Third Publications, 2007), 55.

41. For examples of this process, see chapter 5, "Helping a Person Notice and Share with God Key Interior Facts," in William A. Barry, SJ, and William J. Connolly, SJ, *The Practice of Spiritual Direction* (New York: Seabury Press, 1982). Although the authors' discussion emphasizes an early stage of spiritual direction, it is my experience that many mature and experienced people are also helped by such attentive noticing of religious experience.

42. Lyric poetry is particularly well suited to express an intense experience of brief duration. In the lyric form, the writer condenses into the images and symbols of the poem a highly complex, multivalent reality. Frequently, the lyric deals with a small slice of experience, a momentary awareness or complex perception. Because lyric poetry relies on metaphorical expression as its primary vehicle for conveying meaning, it is strongly tied to the world of actual sense impressions. The poet helps the reader/listener see or experience his or her perception and response to something through the descriptive power of sensory language. Lyric poetry functions directly as an "interpretation of the raw, loose universe." Annie Dillard, *Living by Fiction* (New York: Harper and Row, 1982), 147.

43. Charles Simic, "The Power of Ruins," *The New York Review of Books* (June 22, 2006), 16.

44. Kathleen Fischer, "Working with Emotions in Spiritual Direction: Seven Guiding Principles," *Presence* 12.3 (2006), 31. In this essay Fischer talks about how important it is for directees to recognize and name their feelings because feeling is itself a way of knowing, and transformation often occurs when feelings are acknowledged and put into relationship with God, 26–33.

45. Ignatius of Loyola, *The Spiritual Exercises*, trans. Louis Puhl (Chicago: Loyola University Press, 1951), nos. 190–99.

46. See chapter 1 herein, the section on Mary's experience of retreat direction.

47. This is one form that Ignatius's technique of "repetition" may take. "We should pay attention to and dwell upon those points in which we experienced greater consolation or desolation or greater spiritual appreciation." Puhl, *Exercises*, no. 62.

48. Working with images in this way may not necessarily be an experience of God for everyone. It is, however, a helpful form of meditation for many people and a powerful tool for psychological and spiritual growth; in recent times, Carl G. Jung taught working with images as the process of "active imagination."

49. This is the classical definition of *contemplation* in the Western mystical tradition, which teaches a union in love with God that is characterized by the inability to grasp God by knowledge, imagination, or any activity whatever, but that is available to a person through an obscure, general awareness in knowledge or love or both of God. See John of the Cross, *The Ascent of Mount Carmel*, bks. 11, 13, and 14, in *The Collected Works of St. John of the Cross*, trans. Kieran Kavanaugh and Otilio Rodriguez (Washington, DC: ICS Publications, 1973); or Thomas Merton, *Contemplative Prayer* (New York: Doubleday, 1971), chapter 14, for a series of quotations from the tradition describing and explaining this experience.

50. St. John of the Cross, *Ascent* and *The Dark Night*, in *The Collected Works*; Dionysius the Areopagite, *On the Divine Names and the Mystical Theology*, trans. C. E. Rolt, Translations of Christian Literature, Series 1: Greek Texts (London: SPCK, 1920); *Gregory of Nyssa: The Life of Moses*, trans. Everett Ferguson and Abraham J. Malherbe, Classics of Western Spirituality (New York: Paulist Press, 1978).

51. Teresa of Avila several times distinguishes among different kinds of prayer with comparison to sleep. See chapters 3.11 and 4.86 in *Teresa of Avila: The Interior Castle*, trans. Kieran Kavanaugh, OCD, and Otilio Rodriguez, OCD, Classics of Western Spirituality (New York: Paulist Press, 1979).

52. See John of the Cross, *The Spiritual Canticle*, in *The Collected Works*; Teresa of Avila, *The Interior Castle*; and Pierre Adnés, "Mariage Spirituel," *Dictionnaire de Spiritualité*, vol. 10, cols. 388–408.

53. Carol Eckerman, "Images, Words, and Spiritual Direction," *Presence* 9.2 (2003), 9–14, qtd. at 9.

54. Eckerman, "Images, Words, and Spiritual Direction," 9–10.

55. Amy Tan, *The Opposite of Fate: Memories of a Writing Life* (New York: Penguin, 2003), 322.

56. John Updike, quoted by George Hunt, SJ, in "Updike at Rest," *America* (February 17, 2009), 5.

57. Avery Dulles, *Models of the Church* (New York: Doubleday, 1978), 24–25. I altered the language in this citation into first person plural in order to eliminate the sexist language in the original.

58. Philip Wheelwright, *Metaphor and Reality* (Bloomington, IN: Indiana University Press, 1962), 92–110.

59. See Kathleen Fischer, *The Inner Rainbow: The Imagination in Christian Life* (New York: Paulist Press, 1983), 92–95.

60. Archetypal symbols are those that seem to be universally shared by most people regardless of culture or historical period. These symbols tend to be rooted in everyday human experience in the physical and social world. C. G. Jung drew on these collective patterns in history and culture to formulate his psychological theory of the archetypes and the unconscious. See C. G. Jung, *The Archetypes and the Collective Unconscious*, vol. 9, pt. 1, trans. R. F. C. Hull, The Collected Works of C. G. Jung, Bollingen Series XX (London: Routledge and Kegan Paul, 1959).

61. Bernard Cooke describes personal symbols: "For each of us there are certain things, places, persons, or events that have become especially meaningful and that continue to say something special to us whenever we remember them or encounter them again. In this process of symbols emerging in our consciousness as retainers and transmitters of meaning, a central role is played by our memory. It is because we can recall past happenings, relive them (sometimes with great vividness) in our imagination, reexperience the joy or anguish or achievements of the past, that these can still affect our awareness and our emotions. Along with this, we have the ability, through creative imagination, of sharing vicariously in the meaningful experiences of others. We do this when we see a movie or read a novel or listen to a friend relate a harrowing experience he or she has just passed through. Because symbols have this power to touch the entire range of our consciousness—rational thought, imagination, emotions, dreams—they are a privileged means of expressing our most personal and important and disturbing experiences. The warm handshake of a dear friend, the singing of Christmas carols,...young lovers walking hand in hand, one could go on with a long list of symbols that speak to us on several levels of insight and feeling. Such symbols speak commonly to all of us and yet speak somewhat distinctively to each of us. When we reflect on it, we realize that such symbols do more than express how we think and feel; they are a powerful force in shaping the way we think and feel." Bernard Cooke, *Sacraments and Sacramentality* (Mystic, CT: Twenty-Third Publications, 1983), 44–45.

Chapter 4

1. See James Olney, *Metaphors of the Self: Meaning in Autobiography* (Princeton, NJ: Princeton University Press, 1972.)

2. Thomas Merton, *The Seven Storey Mountain* (New York: Harcourt, Brace and Jovanovich, 1948).

3. "My coming to faith did not start with a leap but rather a series of staggers from what seemed like one safe place to another. Like lily pads, round and green, these places summoned and then held me up while I grew. Each prepared me for the next leaf on which I would land, and in this way I moved across the swamp of doubt and fear. When I look back at some of these early resting places—the boisterous home of the Catholics, the soft armchair of the Christian Science mom, adoption by ardent Jews—I can see how flimsy and indirect a path they made. Yet each step brought me closer to the verdant pad of faith on which I somehow stay afloat today." Anne Lamott, *Traveling Mercies: Some Thoughts on Faith* (New York: Anchor, 2000), 3.

4. Thérèse of Lisieux, *The Story of a Soul: The Autobiography of St. Thérèse of Lisieux*, trans. John Clarke (Washington, DC: Institute of Carmelite Studies, 1972).

5. See George W. Stroup, "The Narrative Form of Personal Identity," in *The Promise of Narrative Theology* (Atlanta: John Knox Press, 1981), 102–5.

6. Peter Collins presents an ethnographic description of this process among Quakers. He found that the "social identity of participants [in the Quaker Meeting] is precipitated in the interplay between three modes of discourse: the…individual, the vernacular [the patterns of the local meeting] and the canonic [key Quaker referential texts]. For individuals to participate successfully in Meeting they are required to present and then reconstruct their autobiographical selves in response to their increasing familiarization both with well-known canonic texts and also the local expression of these texts." "Storying Self and Others: The Construction of Narrative Identity," *Journal of Language and Politics* 2/2 (2003): 251. Downloaded from E-Journals at Fordham University Library, February 16, 2009.

7. Oliver Sacks, a neurosurgeon, poignantly describes the situation of patients who have suffered damage to the part of the brain that supports this narrative construction of identity. Mr. Thompson continually created "…a world and self, to replace what was continually being forgotten and lost. Such a frenzy may call forth brilliant powers of invention and fancy…for such a patient *must literally make himself (and his world) up every moment*. We have each of us,

a life-story, an inner narrative—whose continuity, whose sense, *is* our lives. It might be said that each of us constructs and lives a 'narrative,' and that this narrative *is* us, our identities." *The Man Who Mistook His Wife for a Hat and Other Clinical Tales* (New York: Summit, 1985), 110, italics in the original.

    8. Stroup, *The Promise of Narrative Theology*, 111.

    9. Stroup, *The Promise of Narrative Theology*, 111.

    10. Paul John Eakin, from the first chapter, "Registers of the Self," 1–42, of his *How Our Lives Become Stories: Making Selves* (Ithaca, NY: Cornell University Press, 1999).

    11. Developmental psychologist Ronald Irwin contests the most radical postmodern views that the self is nothing but a socially constructed linguistic creation. He points to a process of maturity that some adults achieve—a postconventional level in which we *have* stories rather than a conventional stage in which we *are* our stories. But he also says that "we begin to intuit a world apart from our symbolically constructed world, *a world beyond language.* The repeated failures to achieve full closure in our cognitive grasping, the continued contradictions thrust on us by our unruly emotions, the failures to predict both ourselves and others, create the ground for repeated experiences of a 'liminal' nature. We begin to notice and acknowledge a new power to act on our world, to change it, and even to step outside of it and walk into totally different and other worlds not of our society's making." He contrasts initial development, which requires adaptation to the natural world (external reality), the psychological world (within ourselves), and the socially constructed cultural world. *Human Development and the Spiritual Life* (Plenum, NY: Kluwer Academic, 2002), 126.

    12. The multiplicity of the self is currently a preoccupation in psychotherapy, especially narrative psychotherapy, and in relational psychoanalysis, both deeply influenced by postmodern theories of the self. See Pamela Cooper-White, *Many Voices: Pastoral Psychotherapy in Relational and Theological Perspectives* (Minneapolis: Fortress, 2006); also see Jill Freedman and Gene Coombs, *Narrative Therapy: The Social Construction of Preferred Realities* (New York: Norton, 1996). These authors emphasize the multiplicity of the self based on different social locations, behaviors, ethnic differences, and unconscious factors. The narrative approach to therapy can be understood as a form of "narrative repair." Therapists coach clients in recognizing the many parts of themselves, both conscious and unconscious, and in constructing a preferred future on this basis. Dan McAdams, among others, contests such a floating sense of self. He wonders, "How many contemporary people actually see themselves as mere locations in time and space rather than as embodied actors with internalized intentions and plans?" He notes, "Some

observers argue that the term *postmodernism* is something of an exaggeration and that recent trends in social life indicate a kind of culmination of modernity...a period of high modernity." McAdams concedes that "the postmodern take on selfhood underscores the difficulty contemporary adults are likely to experience in crafting the reflexive project of the self, especially with regard to their efforts to find a temporal coherence to life through the construction of a self-defining life story." According to McAdams, many "argue that it is a coherent and vivifying life story that best provides the modern adult with that quality of selfhood that goes by the name of *identity*." All citations above are from McAdams, "Personality, Modernity, and the Storied Self: A Contemporary Framework for Studying Persons," *Psychological Inquiry* 7.4 (1996): 299.

13. Ulric Neisser, "Five Kinds of Self-Knowledge," *Philosophical Psychology* 1.1 (1988): 35–59.

14. Neisser, "Five Kinds of Self-Knowledge," 36, including the direct quotation.

15. Neisser, "Five Kinds of Self-Knowledge," 41.

16. Dan P. McAdams et al., "Continuity and Change in the Life Story: A Longitudinal Study of Autobiographical Memories in Emerging Adulthood," *Journal of Personality* 74.5 (October 2006):1371–1400, accessed online from uiuc.edu, March 5, 2009. This research analysis built on the model of personality described in Dan P. McAdams, "The Case for Unity in the (Post)Modern Self," in *Self and Identity*, ed. Richard Ashmore and Lee J. Jossin (New York: Oxford University Press, 1997) and in McAdams et al.; and "Personality, Modernity, and the Storied Self: A Contemporary Framework for Studying Persons," *Psychological Inquiry* 7.4 (1996): 295–321. It is all the more surprising that McAdams finds remarkable continuity of self as well as development in this younger population who is likely to be most influenced by postmodernity and its theories during college years. Herbert J. Hermans focuses on the relational or dialogical self vis-à-vis culture. He, too, asks a question similar to McAdams: "Our present era, often labeled as postmodern, is characterized by an unprecedented intensification of the flow and flux of positions moving in and out of the self space within relatively short time periods. Some intriguing questions can be posed here, such as: does this flow and flux lead to an empty self (Cushman, 1990) or a saturated self (Gergen, 1991) or do they lead to a reorganization of the self in such a way that an intensified flow of positions is counteracted by an increasing need for more stable positions that guarantee a basic consistency of the self-system?" Hermans, "The Dialogical Self: Toward a Theory of Personal and Cultural Positioning," *Culture Psychology* 7.3 (2001): 255, down-

17. Damasio, qtd. in Eakin, *How Our Lives Become Stories*, 31.

18. Antonio Damasio, *The Feeling of What Happens: Body and Emotion in the Making of Consciousness* (New York: Harcourt, 1999), 171–76. A summary from Damasio may help here: "The body-based, dynamic-range stability of the nonconscious proto-self, which is reconstructed live at each instant, and the conscious core self, which emerges from it in the second-order nonverbal account when an object modifies it, are enriched by the accompanying display of memorized and invariant facts—for instance, where you were born, and to whom; critical events in your autobiography; what you like and dislike; your name; and so on. Although the basis for the auto-biographical self is stable and invariant [Crites's "memory stream"], its scope changes continuously as a result of experience. The dis-play of autobiographical self is thus more open to refashioning than the core self, which is reproduced time and again in essentially the same form across a lifetime. Unlike the core self, which inheres as a protagonist of the primordial account, and unlike the proto-self, which is a current representation of the state of the organism, the autobiographical self is based on a concept in the true cognitive and neurobiological sense of the term. The concept exists in the form of dispositional, implicit memories contained in certain intercon-nected brain networks, and many of these implicit memories can be made explicit at any time, simultaneously. Their activation in image form constitutes a backdrop to each moment of a healthy mental life, usually unattended, often just hinted and half guessed, just like the core self and like knowing, and yet there, ready to be made more central if the need arises to confirm that we are who we are. That is the material we use when we describe our personality or the indi-vidual characteristics of another person's mode of being" (173–74). Damasio says we translate these images into language when we tell our stories to ourselves or to another. There is both a strong mea-sure of unity and also of malleability.

19. The directee is Ellen and her spiritual director is Karla. Their dialogue—which shows how this insight unfolded in the ses-sion—is later in this chapter.

20. Daniel Stern, *The Interpersonal World of the Infant* (New York: Basic Books, 1985); Judith Jordan, "The Relational Self: A New Perspective for Understanding Women's Development," *Contem-porary Psychotherapy Review* 7 (1992): 56–72; and Judith Jordan, ed., *Women's Growth in Diversity: More Writings from the Stone Center* (New York: Guilford Press, 1997).

21. Hubert J. M. Hermans poignantly suggests that a dialogical relationship with someone from another culture is particularly sus-

ceptible to misunderstanding. "When people are raised in one culture and then migrate to another, they arrive in a situation in which two or more heterogeneous internal positions (e.g., *I* as Egyptian and *I* as Dutch) interact with a multiplicity of very heterogeneous external positions (e.g., family of one's culture of origin and individuals and groups representing the host culture). Such positions (e.g., Egyptian versus Dutch) may be felt as conflicting or they may coexist in relatively independent ways or even fuse so that hybrid combinations emerge in the form of multiple identities (Hermans & Kempen, 1998). In all these cases there is a high probability of dialogical misunderstanding because the phenomenon of multiple identities raises the challenging question how people, involved in a process of acculturation, organize and reorganize their self-system in such a way that they are able to share with other people cultural elements that may be highly divergent, partly unknown and laden with power differences." Hermans, "The Dialogical Self," 258. It is very important for spiritual directors working cross-culturally to take these possibilities into account and to try to join with such a directee empathically, even though the directee's thinking and feeling arise from a different internal and cultural process than from one's own.

22. Steven Marcus gives an interesting account of the correlation of narrative accuracy with mental health in Freud's famous Case of Dora. "...Freud is implying that a coherent story is in some manner connected with mental health....On this reading, human life is, ideally, a connected and coherent story, with all the details in explanatory place, and with everything (or as close to everything as is practically possible) accounted for, in its proper causal or other sequence. And inversely, illness amounts at least in part to suffering from an incoherent story or an inadequate narrative account of oneself." Steven Marcus, "Freud and Dora: Story, History, Case History," in *Representations: Essays on Literature and Society* (New York: Random House, 1975), 276–77.

23. Jung prefers another story: "In many cases in psychiatry, the patient who comes to us has a story that is not told, and which as a rule no one knows of. To my mind, therapy only really begins after the investigation of that wholly personal story. It is the patient's secret, the rock against which he is shattered. If I know his secret story, I have a key to the treatment." C. G. Jung, *Memories, Dreams, and Reflections*, recorded and ed. Aniela Jaffe, trans. Richard and Clara Winston, 4th ed. (New York: Vintage, 1965), 117.

24. John Navone and Thomas Cooper, *Tellers of the Word* (New York: Le Jacq, 1981), 105.

25. John S. Dunne, *The Mystic Road of Love* (Notre Dame, IN: Univ. of Notre Dame Press, 1999), 32–34.

26. Feminist criticism of psychoanalytic theory and feminist theory of autobiography indicate that women's ego consciousness differs from that of men. Women tend to develop ego boundaries that are more permeable than men's. Their identities develop in such a way that they include service to others without threat to their own identities. In addition, because of a greater variety of social roles that women enact simultaneously, their autobiographies generally reflect what men would consider to be a fragmented consciousness rather than a highly unified one. Women tend to prefer the diary form, which better represents their experience than the autobiography organized around a single dominant theme or role. See Jean Baker Miller, "Serving Others' Needs—Doing for Others," in *Toward a New Psychology of Women* (Boston: Beacon Press, 1978); and Carol Gilligan, *In a Different Voice* (Cambridge, MA: Harvard University Press, 1982), for the psychological theory. For a feminist theory of autobiography, see Estelle C. Jelinek, "Introduction: Women's Autobiography and the Male Tradition," in *Women's Autobiography: Essays in Criticism*, ed. Estelle Jelinek (Bloomington, IN: Indiana University Press, 1980), 1–20; and Mary G. Mason, "The Other Voice: Autobiographies of Women Writers," in *Autobiography: Essays Theoretical and Critical*, ed. James Olney (Princeton, NJ: Princeton University Press, 1980), 207–35.

27. Autobiographies are usually written only by those whose lives illuminate the issues, politics, philosophies, and so on, of a given period of history in such a way that makes their lives significant for others. Critical studies of autobiography indicate that to tell one's own story is an act of self-assertion that claims the right to define oneself. Socially disenfranchised groups tend to be rendered invisible as well as defined by the ways the enfranchised describe them in their stories. Through the opportunity to tell their story to someone who "counts" in their eyes, ordinary or marginalized people discover that they have a valuable story to tell. Elizabeth Winston, "The Autobiographer and Her Readers: From Apology to Affirmation," in *Women's Autobiography*, 93–111. Anthropologist Barbara Myerhoff documents the effect of storytelling for members of a senior citizens' center. Myerhoff, "Telling One's Story," *The Center Magazine* (March 1980): 22–23.

28. Leigh Gilmore, "Policing Truth: Confession, Gender, and Autobiographical Authority," in *Autobiography and Postmodernism*, ed. Kathleen Ashley, Leigh Gilmore, and Gerald Peters (Amherst, MA: Univ. of Massachusetts Press, 1994), 60–62. Gilmore describes the constraints of women mystics who wrote under the critical eye of a confessor. The confessor determined if visions were of delusional (today labeled mental illness), diabolic, or divine origins. If the confessor authenticated the vision, the woman was authorized in her

religious role. If a vision was judged to be diabolic, the visionary might undergo procedures such as exorcism or be put to death as a witch by the Inquisition. On the other hand, these women felt empowered to speak and claim spiritual power because of their mystical experience with God.

29. John M. Staudenmaier thinks that the narrative dimension of spiritual direction can help to counteract the negative influence of technology in our culture. *Studies in the Spirituality of Jesuits* 19 (1987): 32–33.

30. Betty Bergland, "Postmodernism and the Autobiographical Subject," in *Autobiography and Postmodernism*, 130.

31. See Roy W. Fairchild, *Lifestory Conversations* (New York: United Presbyterian Church., U.S.A., 1977), 14–15: "Memory serves our sense of identity and continuity. To understand where we have been contributes to an understanding of where we are now and where we are going....Each person is living out a unique, never to be repeated story. Unless one can survey accomplishments, regrets, high points and low points of past experience, the celebrations and the wildernesses, one cannot begin to perceive how God has been working in his/her story....It is possible that a life which has been viewed as simply a series of individual happenings—as fragments, splinters, and broken off pieces—can be joined together in conversation by a thread of meaning that runs through them all." Also see anthropologist Barbara Myerhoff's account of the effect of storytelling for members of a senior citizens' center. Myerhoff, "Telling One's Story," *The Center Magazine* (March 1980): 22–23. Life reviews in oral and written forms have become standard programs in senior citizens' centers. More recent books that offer step-by-step directions for life-story writing are Richard L. Morgan, *Remembering Your Story: Creating Your Own Spiritual Autobiography* (Nashville: Upper Room, 2002); and Bill Roorbach, *Writing Life Stories: How to Make Memories into Memoirs* (Cincinnati, OH: Writer's Digest Books, 2008).

32. Robert McAfee Brown suggests that most people live plural stories, some of which may conflict with the story God is trying to author with us in our lives: "I not only am many stories, but I *have* many stories. I am constantly balancing—or juggling—a number of ways *of* telling my own story: the masculine version, the American version, the human version, the Christian version, the university professor version, and so on. But I am also constantly reviewing those stories of my time: the feminine version, the Black version, the Third World version, the Jewish version, the blue collar version....Within this multitude *of* stories, I accord one story, or several stories, a higher authority than others....If things go well, my normative story is authenticated....But things may not go well. My normative story may be...so badly challenged or shattered that I must

painfully reconstruct a new story for myself," from "My Story and 'the Story,'" *Theology Today* 32 (July 1975): 167. This theme will be treated in more detail as the "discernment of stories."

33. Carolyn Gratton, *Guidelines for Spiritual Direction*, Studies in Formative Spirituality, vol. 3 (Denville, NJ: Dimension Books, 1980), 106.

34. Brennan Manning, *A Stranger to Self-Hatred* (Denville, NJ: Dimension Books, 1982), 95.

35. See John Shea, *An Experience Named Spirit* (Chicago: Thomas More Press, 1983), beginning on 102 for an extended discussion of this process.

36. See Stroup, *The Promise of Narrative Theology*, 116–17.

37. John Shea, *An Experience Named Spirit*, 109.

38. See Ignatius of Loyola, *The Exercises*, nos. 113, 36; and Ernest Larkin, *Silent Presence: Discernment as Process and Problem* (Denville, NJ: Dimension, 1981).

39. See Jerome Neufelder and Mary Coelho, *Writings on Spiritual Direction by Great Christian Masters* (New York: Seabury Press, 1982), 117–24, for several classical and contemporary writers on the theme of self-knowledge and its importance in the spiritual life.

40. Eakin, *How Our Lives Become Stories*, particularly chapter 2, "Relational Selves, Relational Lives," 43–98.

41. Tad Dunne, *Spiritual Mentoring: Guiding People through Spiritual Exercises to Life Decisions* (San Francisco: HarperSanFrancisco, 1991), 21.

42. Tad Dunne, *Spiritual Mentoring*, 21.

43. Tad Dunne, *Spiritual Mentoring*, 21.

44. Ray Hart, *Unfinished Man and the Imagination: Toward an Ontology and a Rhetoric of Revelation* (Atlanta: Scholars Press, 1985), 253–54.

45. Frederick S. Perls, *Gestalt Therapy Verbatim* (Lafayette, CA: Real People Press, 1969).

46. "It is a question of the form of attention we choose to bestow; of our willingness to see that in reading according to restricted codes we disregard as noise what, if read differently, patiently, would make another and rarer kind of sense." Frank Kermode, *The Genesis of Secrecy: On the Interpretation of Narrative* (Cambridge, MA: Harvard Univ. Press, 1979), 96. For an example of feminist criticism that reads the "secrets" in fiction by women writers, see Susan M. Gilbert and Susan Gubar, *Madwomen in the Attic* (New Haven. CT: Yale University Press, 1979).

47. Frederick Buechner, *Telling Secrets: A Memoir* (San Francisco: HarperSanFranciso, 1991), 3.

48. Daniel De Roulet, *Finding Your Plot in a Plotless World: A Little Direction* (Grand Rapids, MI: Brazos Press, 2007), 34–35.

49. Since suggesting another ending to someone else's story may also inhibit a tentative directee, the director needs to be careful. When I begin to hear a repetitive pattern that indicates the directee is unknowingly stuck in a negative story, I find it helpful to propose a variety of possible outcomes rather than only one alternative. This encourages the directee to entertain an alternative outcome without feeling pressured to adopt one of my suggestions.

50. According to Paul Ricoeur, "To follow a story, then, is to understand the successive actions, thoughts, and feelings as having a *particular directedness*. By this I mean that we are pulled forward by the development and respond to this thrust with expectations concerning the outcome and the ending of the whole process. In this sense, the 'conclusion' of the story is the attracting pole of the process. But a narrative conclusion can be neither deduced nor predicted. No story without surprises, coincidences, encounters, revelations, recognitions, etc., would hold our attention. This is why we have to follow it *to the conclusion.* Instead of being predictable, a conclusion must be acceptable. Looking backward from the conclusion over the episodes that led up to it, we must be able to say that this end required those events and this chain of actions. Yet this backward glance is made possible by the teleologically guided movement of our expectations when we followed the story." "The Narrative Function," *Semeia* 13 (1978): 182.

51. It's important to emphasize that the material in this chapter about and by Mary was the result of my interview with her. This interview took place some time *after* she had written her account of the retreat, and the account itself was not written until *three years after the retreat.* Keep this timing in mind—retreat, followed by account, followed by interview—to see how Mary continues to shape and reflect on this particular story.

52. Working with symbols that arise from the directee's narrative may be enhanced in a number of ways. Psychosynthesis, as developed by Roberto Assagioli, *Psychosynthesis* (New York: Penguin, 1971), encourages people to visualize symbols that will foster their integration and development. One of the classic visualizations for cultivating spiritual development is the life cycle of the rose from seed to fully opened flower. Assagioli, 214ff. See also Piero Ferucci, *What We May Be* (Los Angeles: Tarcher, 1982), 117ff, for further development of this topic. If a director responds to images that emerge in the directee by suggesting visualization or painting, discernment is required in order to decide whether the effect of an image needs to be intensified or lessened. Images bear within them the possibility of encouraging development or regression.

53. Wesley Kort, *Narrative Elements and Religious Meaning* (Philadelphia: Fortress Press, 1975), 35.

54. A more extensive discussion of narrated experiences of mystery and their importance in spiritual-direction narratives will be taken up in chapter 5.

55. Opal, the spiritual director-in-training, was a person in recovery; hence the references to a High Power. She was also married to a Hindu from India; hence the references to Hindu and Buddhist stories and philosophies.

56. Hans-Georg Gadamer, *Truth and Method*, trans. and ed. Garrett Barden and John Cumming, from the 1965 ed. (New York: Crossroad, 1975), 252.

57. The historical survey of the models of spiritual direction in the introduction suggests something of the richness and conflicting variety in the tradition on this topic.

Chapter 5

1. See Gerard Egan, *The Skilled Helper* (Monterey, CA: Brookes/Cole Publishing, 1975), 106–8, for an explanation of social influence theory.

2. Narrative psychologists intend to influence their clients to change their stories or to develop a future story out of a submerged or forgotten plot from the past. "Our intention, then, is not to co-construct stories that represent or describe experience, but to co-construct stories through which people can live in preferred ways....Returning to an event in her life on which she performed meaning was the childhood experience of sitting on her grandmother's lap and teaching her grandmother a song. Jessica immersed herself in that memory and saw herself through her grandmother's eyes. Then she developed the story through time, authoring and experiencing a speculative history of what her life would have been like if she had lived with her grandmother. After this conversation, Jessica found herself doing a whole range of things that were unusual, from saying 'thank you' to quitting smoking. She said that she had gained an understanding through our work of the kind of person she was and was being the person she now knew she was. She began living a new story, not simply telling it. The story was both shaped by life events and shaping of life events and self image." Jill Freedman and Gene Combs, *Narrative Therapy: The Social Construction of Preferred Realities* (New York: W. W. Norton, 1996), 88.

3. Carolyn Gratton, *Guidelines to Spiritual Direction*, Studies in Formative Spirituality. vol. 3 (Denville, NJ: Dimension Books, 1980), 171–72.

4. I am indebted to Professor Francis Houdek, SJ, for this insight about the discovery of God in the search for self as it takes place in the context of spiritual direction. He said to me in an interview (Berkeley, CA, January 18, 1985): "I think people come to direction with two reasons that get verbalized. And if direction goes with any fruitfulness, they find out the two reasons are the same. They come either to find themselves or to find God. And they work at direction from either one of those two perspectives. When they find themselves, they find God is very present. When they really discover God, in that whole process they find themselves."

5. Ronald R. Irwin, *Human Development and the Spiritual Life* (New York: Kluswer Academic / Plenum Publishers, 2002), 7.

6. Irwin, *Human Development and the Spiritual Life*, 19.

7. Roy Schafer, a neo-Freudian psychoanalyst, offers a particularly illuminating description of the storytelling process in psychoanalysis that captures both similarities to the narrative situation of spiritual direction and significant differences: "We narrate others just as we narrate selves. The other person, like the self, is not something one has or encounters as such but an existence one tells. Consequently, telling 'others' about 'ourselves' is doubly narrative. Often the stories we tell about ourselves are historical or autobiographical; we locate them in the past. For example, one might say, 'Until I was fifteen, I was proud of my father' or 'I had a totally miserable childhood.' These histories are present tellings. The same may be said of the histories we attribute to others. We change many implied or stated questions to which they are the answer. As a project in personal development, personal analysis changes the leading questions that one addresses to the tale of one's life and the lives of important others. People going through psychoanalysis, analysands, tell the analyst about themselves and others in the past and present. In making interpretations, the analyst retells these stories. In the retelling, certain features are accentuated while others are placed in parentheses; certain features are related to others in new ways or for the first time; some features are developed further, perhaps at great length. This retelling is done along psychoanalytic lines." Roy Schafer, *The Analytic Attitude* (New York: Basic Books, 1983), 219.

8. One directee expressed a feeling of relief and joy at being able to explore explicitly the spiritual dimension of his experience. He had been in therapy for two years and reported that he could not explore the spiritual or moral dimension of his midlife crisis within the counseling situation because the therapist would not respond to this aspect of his experience. Although he could introduce the material, the therapist's nonengagement with it frustrated his attempts to incorporate his story of faith into his therapeutic story in that narrative situation.

9. Jill Ker Conway, *When Memory Speaks: Reflections on Autobiography* (New York: Alfred Knopf, 1998), 176.

10. Robert Scholes and Robert Kellogg, *The Nature of Narrative* (New York: Oxford University Press, 1966), 157.

11. Barrett J. Mandel, "Full of Life Now," in *Autobiography: Essays Theoretical and Critical*, ed. James Olney (Princeton, NJ: Princeton University Press, 1980), 64.

12. Formal autobiographies are "generally silent on intense feelings of hate, love, and fear, the disclosure of explicit sexual encounters, or the detailing of painful psychological experience." Estelle C. Jelinek, "Introduction to Women's Autobiography and the Male Tradition," in *Women's Autobiography: Essays in Criticism*, ed. Estelle C. Jelinek (Bloomington, IN: Indiana University Press, 1980), 17.

13. See Friedrich Wulf, "Spiritual Direction," in *Sacramentum Mundi*, vol. 6 (New York: Herder and Herder, 1968–70), 166; and Francis Kelly Nemeck and Marie Theresa Coombs, *The Way of Spiritual Direction*, Consecrated Life Series, vol. 5 (Wilmington, DE: Michael Glazier, 1985), 81.

14. Wolfgang Iser describes the concept of the implied reader: "The concept of the implied reader is...a textual structure anticipating the presence of a recipient without necessarily defining him: This concept prestructures the role to be assumed by each recipient, and this holds true even when texts deliberately appear to ignore their possible recipient or actively exclude him. Thus the concept of the implied reader designates a network of response-inviting structures, which impel the reader to grasp the text. No matter who or what he may be, the real reader is always offered a particular role to play, and it is this role that constitutes the concept of the implied reader." Wolfgang Iser, *The Act of Reading: A Theory of Aesthetic Response* (Baltimore, MD: Johns Hopkins University Press, 1978), 34–35. See also Wayne C. Booth, *The Rhetoric of Fiction*, 2nd ed. (Chicago: University of Chicago Press, 1983), chapters 5 and 6.

15. Recent studies in the narrative construction of identity reinforce this same point. Stanton Wortham describes not only the representational characteristic of oral autobiography, which tends to reinforce the established story but also shows the interactional positioning interviewees engage in. The story is always being told to a particular person and reinforces the kind of person the teller wants to represent. At the same time, the storyteller is also enacting this story in relationship to the other person in the dialogue. "Interactional Positioning and Narrative Self-Construction," *Narrative Inquiry* 10 (2000): 157–84.

16. See Iser, *The Act of Reading*, 96, for a discussion of the way textual segments are presented to the reader's viewpoint in such a

way that the reader becomes actively involved in constructing the connections between seemingly unrelated segments of the narrative.

17. "The artful diarist who senses a kind of plot in his or her life will be selecting appropriate materials 'half-consciously.'" Scholes and Kellogg, *The Nature of Narrative*, 211.

18. Iser identifies four textual perspectives: narrator, character, plot, and reader. At any one moment, one of these perspectives takes center stage. Iser calls the momentary focus on such a perspective a "theme." A "theme," however, is always set against a "horizon," which in this case encompasses all the other perspectives with which one was previously engaged. Iser, *The Act of Reading*, 96–97.

19. Scholes and Kellogg categorize "slice of life" and cinema verité as empirical and mimetic forms of narration. They belong to representational narrative tending to emphasize mimesis more than plot. Scholes and Kellogg, *The Nature of Narrative*, 13.

20. Sholes and Kellogg, *The Nature of Narrative*, 27.

21. Scholes and Kellogg trace this cultural interest in the inward development of character as a primarily Christian element in our narrative literature. *The Nature of Narrative*, 165. It seems as if the director and perhaps the directee as well can construct this type of meaning for these narratives because they have already learned to follow this type of plot in their experience of novels.

22. Iser asserts that "blanks" that cause a suspension of connectability in a story stimulate the reader's imagination. Serials, which calculate the location of a cut, deliberately prolong the tension. "The result is that we try to imagine how the story will unfold, and in this way we heighten our own participation in the course of events." Iser, *The Act of Reading*, 191. The nature of spiritual-direction narratives creates this kind of suspense because directees are telling sacred tales that have not yet ended. The imaginative participation of the director in the directee's stories can tempt a director to satisfy his or her curiosity about an unresolved plot line. This curiosity could interfere with the directee's freedom to tell the story he or she needs to tell after the lapse of time between sessions.

23. Estelle Jelinek, "Introduction," 17.

24. Mary Catherine Bateson proposes in *Composing A Life* (New York: Penguin, 1990) that women's autobiographies are more like jazz improvisations than linear story lines, because of the way even professional women's careers are interrupted by a greater variety of circumstances than are men's lives. This requires them to improvise new themes in response to these vicissitudes. [This note within the quotation is mine and is not in the original.]

25. Suzanne Juhasz, "Towards a Theory of Form in Feminist Autobiography: Kate Millett's *Flying* and *Sita*; Maxine Hong Kingston's *The Woman Warrior*," in *Women's Autobiography*, 223.

26. Spiritual director Paul Janowiak, SJ, offered his lively description of the way he experienced the difference between men's and women's narratives (author interview, Berkeley, CA, December 14, 1984):

Paul: There is more control in men's stories, whereas a woman will tend to go off into the clear blue yonder, like talking about a flower. A man would be more reticent to talk that way. Men don't refer to themselves in organic images that often. Women's stories tend to be more fused with nature images and less controlled.

Interviewer: Do they seem to you to be more rambling, less coherent?

Paul: No, it's just that they will interject feelings into the experience more. I think men tend to report the experience more as it happened. Men tend to report actions. He said this, and then I said that. He did this and I did that, etc.

Interviewer: When they tell you what happened, do they tend to use metaphors?

Paul: What comes to mind is that it is more common for me to hear women say: it was as if I were a flower and I was opening up. I don't remember men using that kind of imagery as often as women. A man would be more likely to say, "I guess I'm becoming more mature" as opposed to "I feel myself kind of opening up."

27. When I began to tell my own story in direction, I often felt I provided more detail than the directors probably needed. I, however, didn't see how they could help me if I did not convey my complete experience to them. When I condensed my stories to summaries, I questioned my motives for selecting the particular omissions. If I left out what was confusing, then there was nothing for which I needed help. I believed that I had to give some sense of the whole quality of my diverse experiences for the director to understand. Only after two years of regular direction did I begin to discover what I could omit, although I continue to prefer sharing a vivid sense of the multidimensionality of my life in a richly detailed narrative. What seemed to be happening to me in these conversa-

tions was the opportunity to name my own reality and trust my experience. It marked the awakening of my own feminist conscious-ness as I experienced the freedom to tell myself (construct my unique identity) and tell my sacred stories. See Carol Christ on the importance of such storytelling for women, *Diving Deep and Surfacing: Women Writers on Spiritual Quest* (Boston: Beacon, 1980).

28. This phrase comes from a poem by Emily Dickinson in which she says: "Tell all the Truth but tell it slant— / Success in Circuit lies." Emily Dickinson, Poem #426 (1126), *Final Harvest*, ed. Thomas H. Johnson (Boston: Little, Brown, and Company, 1964), 248.

29. Karl Rahner, *Foundations of Christian Faith*, trans. William V. Dych (New York: Crossroad, 1981), 60–67.

30. Denis Edwards, *Human Experience of God* (New York: Paulist Press, 1983), 28.

31. John Shea, *Stories of God* (Chicago: Thomas More, 1978), 24–25.

32. William J. Bausch in *Storytelling: Imagination and Faith* (Mystic, CT: Twenty-Third Publications, 1984) collects a large num-ber of such stories from a variety of sources as he also does in *Touching the Heart* (Mystic, CT: Twenty-Third Publications, 2007); Megan McKenna, *Parables: The Arrows of God* (Ossining, NY: Maryknoll, 1994); and Joy Carol, *Journeys of Courage: Remarkable Stories of the Healing Power of Community* (Notre Dame, IN: Sorin Books, 2003).

33. Edwards, *Human Experience of God*, 27.

34. Henri Nouwen describes something similar when he wrote about the way loneliness might open into a rich experience of soli-tude. Henri Nouwen, *Reaching Out* (Garden City, NY: Doubleday, 1975). John S. Dunne writes extensively about discovering we are not alone even at times when we suffer rejection or the absence of a beloved. Dunne writes, "That is what I feel about the journey with God in time: my joy in the journey is strengthened or encouraged by the presence of God, who is my companion on the way. Listening to God tell my story means being receptive to this joy, this strength-ening, this encouragement. It is true, listening I am learning God is my companion and not a human being, visible and tangible. There is joy here and there is sadness." *The Mystic Road of Love* (Notre Dame, IN: Notre Dame University Press, 1999), 36.

35. John Shea, *Stories of Faith* (Chicago: Thomas More, 1980), 15.

36. According to Joseph Powers, "Since life stories are human stories, they are stories of a truth not yet in complete possession, but a truth to be found in fidelity to the search for the meaning of

life in the face of the death which confronts every human." In "The Art of Believing," *Theological Studies* 39 (December 1978): 664.

37. Shea, *Stories of Faith*, 29.

38. Shea, *Stories of Faith*, 29, 32–33.

39. Author interviews with James and Carmen Neafsey (Berkeley, CA, February 28, 1985) and with Francis Houdek, SJ (Berkeley, CA, January 18, 1985). These three directors were particularly aware of the change in narrational style. Frank Houdek also pointed out that, by contrast, a facile use of religious jargon to describe a "God experience" might indicate the directee was using "God-talk" to evade or control an encounter with mystery.

40. Janet K. Ruffing, "The World Transfigured: Kataphatic Religious Experience Explored through Qualitative Research Methodology," *Studies in Spirituality* 5 (1995): 232–59.

Conclusion

1. Amy Tan, *The Opposite of Fate: Memories of a Writing Life* (New York: Penguin, 2003), 354.

2. This truth is neither the directee's alone nor the director's, but "transcends the subjective opinions of the partners." Hans-Georg Gadamer, *Truth and Method* (New York: Crossroad, 1975), 331.

3. Gadamer, *Truth and Method*, 321.

4. Gadamer, *Truth and Method*, 321–22.

5. Gadamer, *Truth and Method*, 322.

6. Gadamer, *Truth and Method*, 23. In this case, the director's "own self-awareness consists precisely in his [her] withdrawing from the dialectic of this reciprocity, in his [her] reflecting himself [herself] out of his [her] relation to the other and so becoming unreachable by him [her]. By understanding the other, by claiming to know him [her], one takes from him [her] all justification of his [her] own claims. The dialectic of charitable or welfare work in particular operates in this way, penetrating all relationships between men [and women] as a reflective form of the effort to dominate. The claim to understand the other person in advance performs the function of keeping the claim of the other person at a distance." Pages 353–54.

7. Gadamer, *Truth and Method*, 324.

8. Interview with Paul Janowiak (Berkeley, December 14, 1985). Jim Neafsey described something similar when he and his wife Carmen were reflecting on their doing spiritual direction as a couple. "The...thing I feel, I know that Carmen has felt this too, is the experience of God during that hour with a person. It is kind of like

a mini-conversion during our day, calling us to be present to God. This is something we have seen together, especially as a couple. We are together more than we would ordinarily be, and in a more peaceful place, a place where we are mutually participating in God's presence." Interview with James and Carmen Neafsey (Berkeley, February 28, 1985).

9. John Shea, *Stories of Faith* (Chicago: Thomas More Press, 1980), 24–25.

10. Wolfgang Iser, *The Act of Reading: A Theory of Aesthetic Response* (Baltimore, MD: Johns Hopkins University Press, 1978), 35.

11. See particularly Paul John Eakin, ed., *The Ethics of Life Writing* (Ithaca, NY: Cornell University Press, 2004). Within this volume, John Barbour's essay, "Judging and Not Judging Parents," 73–98, explores the sensitive areas of moral interpretation, compassionate understanding of self and parents, and ultimately forgiveness as an outcome of life writing.

12. Roy Schafer, *The Analytic Attitude* (New York: Basic Books, 1983), 219.

13. Paul Elie, *The Life You Save May Be Your Own: An American Pilgrimage* (New York: Farrar, Straus, and Giroux, 2003), 472.